MAINE BOY GOES TO WAR

&

THE STORY OF MIZPAH

A Memoir By Paul Marshall

Published by

LEGACY PRESERVES

www.legacypreserves.com

ISBN-13: 978-1500979201

ISBN-10: 1500979201

Edited by Meghan Vigeant of Legacy Preserves
Book and cover design by Amy Wilder Files of wilderbydesign

THE ROAD NOT TAKEN

Two roads diverged in a yellow wood,
And sorry I could not travel both
And be one traveler, long I stood
And looked down one as far as I could
To where it bent in the undergrowth;

Then took the other, as just as fair,
And having perhaps the better claim,
Because it was grassy and wanted wear;
Though as for that the passing there
Had worn them really about the same,

And both that morning equally lay
In leaves no step had trodden black.
Oh, I kept the first for another day!
Yet knowing how way leads on to way,
I doubted if I should ever come back.

I shall be telling this with a sigh
Somewhere ages and ages hence:
Two roads diverged in a wood, and I—
I took the one less traveled by,
And that has made all the difference.

Robert Frost

Contents

Part III: The Story of Mizpah

Introduction

People have asked me why I chose *Maine Boy Goes to War* as the title of my book. As a World War II veteran I find myself connected with people all over the country. Wherever I go I meet veterans and their families. I sometimes wear a cap with the title of my infantry division on it, which often prompts folks to thank me and ask questions about my service.

Many people know about WWII, but few know what it feels like to be in a war, to see people killed or wounded, to witness the total destruction of cities, towns, and homes. Children of veterans often say to me, "My father was in the war, but he never talked about it." Most of us who saw the horrors of war simply want to forget about it. When we begin to talk it becomes real to us again. I wanted to tell the story of my war experiences in such a way that the loved ones of a war veteran can have a better understanding of what we combat veterans have tried to forget.

Most of us who went off to war were very young men. Millions of us had just turned 18 years of age when we were drafted, called into service whether we wanted to go or not.

We were boys, just finishing high school. My idyllic boyhood in the woods of northern Maine ended, and likewise the innocence of youth came to an abrupt stop for all of us. We left the comfort and loving care of our homes and families. We were taught to kill. The thought that we might not come home again went through our minds when we boarded a troop ship headed for combat. My story is the story of millions of us who took the Oath of Allegiance, that "if necessary, we would be willing to give our lives."

There were many times when memories of my childhood in northern Maine brought me great comfort during the war. In training, I had a difficult time understanding why the officers were so harsh; my family had offered me only love, guidance, and freedom. I had to confront a whole new world order in the army. When I was hiding out in the remains of shelled-out houses in Europe, I had a few occasions to put my farm skills to work to help keep my platoon nourished and happy. Those were rare opportunities, but they warmed my Maine boy heart all the more.

Years after the war I jumped at a chance to bring a message of love and empowerment to a downtrodden people in the islands of the Pacific. My family and I took on the roles of missionaries in a very different culture in Micronesia. We built a high school from the ground up and created a curriculum to rival a quality American education. Here was an opportunity to teach young people how to become leaders of their country, to turn the tide of destruction into something good. It was an experience that shaped my family and me nearly as much, if not more, than our students.

These stories of my life have all come from my memory library, which seems to be a living breathing thing. If any of my memories do not match with others' memories of such events, please bear in mind that memory can play tricks on us all at times. I have shared these stories in honesty and truth to the best of my knowledge.

I have always enjoyed storytelling and reading books to my children. I never thought that someday I might tell my own story, but as I have moved through life, people have expressed interest in my story. A stranger I might tell some of my tales to would remark: "Why don't you put that in a book?" With that positive prompting, I have finally followed those suggestions.

I hope you enjoy my story of a Maine boy who confronts war and goes on to share a message of love.

PART I: A MAINE BOY

Gone Up River: Dad's Story

My father, Joseph Henry Marshall, was the youngest of 11 children, born on a family farm in Millville, New Brunswick, Canada. He worked from the time he was a child and left home to find his way in the world at the age of 14. Two of his older sisters left home and found work and husbands in Boston. They wanted to help their youngest brother so they sent for him to come to Boston and go to trade school. Soon after his arrival in Boston, his sisters located a school for mechanics, programmed to train young men to work on the "Els" (elevated trains) of Boston that were beginning to flourish there.

He attended the school somewhat reluctantly and learned to be a trolley conductor, but he missed the woods of New Brunswick. For a country boy, Boston was noisy and crowded. Friendless and lonely, as one can be among crowds, Dad longed for the smells of spruce and fir, the whispering pines of the deep woods, the roaring and the rushing of the spring torrents. An increasing gnawing finally led him north on the train headed home.

When his train reached Bangor, Maine he started to run out of money and needed to find a way to earn more. There he met a man who told him about the woods camps in northern Maine. He convinced my dad this might be just what he was looking for.

"How do I get there, and how do I get a job?" he asked his new friend.

"There's a place right near the station hiring men for woods camps. If they hire you, they pay your way to the worksite."

What more could anyone wish? Soon he found himself with a ticket on a train headed north. Upon arriving at Sherman Station, he had to walk nine miles to Patten. From there, he could get a ride all the way to the camp, which was 45 miles away. Can you imagine how he must have felt?

His biggest problem was all he had for clothes were the few he had when he lived in Boston. Some were warm enough for the city, but no way would they serve for the Maine woods. He had also been told that

Grandfather Herbert Boynton's logging camp, Crystal, Maine, 1911

a store in Patten carried all the winter clothes that a woodsman might need. But Dad only had $10 left to his name.

Dad entered the store carrying only a ragged suitcase his sister gave him, although it contained practically nothing of value. The storeowner, Mr. Rowe, I believe his name was, outfitted him with the gear he needed.

My father said, "All I've got is $10."

Mr. Rowe said, "Just leave your suitcase here and when you come out in the spring you can pay me what you owe and pick up your suitcase."

When the stage arrived, Dad climbed aboard with a new pair of boots, two sets of long johns, two flannel shirts, a sweater, two pairs of mittens, wool socks, a pipe and enough tobacco to supply a man until he could earn enough to buy more from the camp store.

That story could well be told about many a woodsman and people who helped them back in the days when a handshake was better than a signature. Trust in northern Maine was a natural thing for most everyone.

Early on, Maine became famous for its "broad arrow" pine trees, those tall, stately and sturdy trees, ideal for ships masts. The name *broad*

Grandpa's Logging Camp, Crystal, Maine, 1911

arrow came from the practice of emblazing an arrow on the trunk of the trees so no one but the king's foresters would be able to take them down. During the 1800s and early 1900s, men came from about everywhere to cut logs in Maine. Many young men, like my father and two of his older brothers, came from Canada. In the logging camps you could often hear a mixture of languages and accents from Ireland, France, Poland and Russia, places where there was sometimes very little employment.

Men went "up river" to cut the logs and then "down river" to "drive" them to the sawmills. From there, the lumber was shipped to some far-off destination to build an ever-growing America. When I was a boy we'd say things like, "Jim's gone up river" or "He's gone down river," and folks knew what you meant.

Dad caught the stagecoach and went deep into the woods in early September. He lived in a log cabin at Eagle Lake, about 80 miles north of Patten. My dad worked as a chopper in the days before chain saws. Choppers knew how to undercut and then chop into a tree so that it fell exactly where they wanted it so a horse or oxen could "twitch" it to the landing on the riverside.

In the spring, as soon as the ice gave way and heavy currents of water could carry the logs along, the drive began. Many of the loggers went right along with the logs, working the sides of the rivers and streams pushing, coaxing, often with a few chosen words to help force the logs along to their destination.

Occasionally logs would snag with an unmovable rock or ledge and pile up, causing a jam. If the river drivers couldn't get that key log to move they had to resort to TNT, dynamite. It was tricky and dangerous, and many a driver riding the logs would get caught as he tried to escape the blast and sudden shifting of logs headed down river. That's how my Uncle Gideon died while driving logs in New Hampshire.

Dad started out his work in the woods camp that first summer as the cook. The men in the logging camps relied on barrels of flour, molasses, salt pork, eggs and beef to feed them through the winter. Deer and moose were plentiful in the woods and usually one man's entire job was to provide enough deer and moose for 50 men or more. Salt pork was a most useful food product as it was used in all sorts of cooking. It was also the base for soups and anything requiring some fat content. It was the only source of grease for pancakes, a staple at a woods camp breakfast. There was often a contest in a logging camp to see who could put away the largest number of pancakes in one sitting.

My dad used to tell us how they'd use salt pork barrels in the camps after the pork was gone. Occasionally, a man died in a woods camp, from an accident or sickness. Many of them were buried right outside the camp, but they couldn't bury them in the wintertime when the ground was frozen. Usually there was a family waiting back home for their loved one's body to return. So they'd put the body into the brine of an empty salt pork barrel, which preserved it until they could bring him back to his family. I always wondered if my father made this story up. Woodsmen often liked to tell stories and were usually very good at it. It was a good pastime when they were sitting around the camp stove after their 12-hour work day, but some of those stories had to be taken with a grain of salt, as the saying goes.

My father came out of the Maine woods in April when the logs were driven down river. He had to find work for the summer and the town of Patten looked like a good choice. Many loggers and camp supplies came through there. The farmers of Patten provided potatoes, turnips, beets, carrots, cabbages, onions, and cornmeal for the loggers, plus oats and straw for the workhorses. Those farmers needed workers too.

Dad could always find work. He was known as a good worker. He worked in several places in the summers and finally came to Herb Boynton's Katahdin Valley Farm. Herb needed a hired man, room and board included, to help farm, clear the land, and work in his logging camp. That fit my dad, who, although still in his teens, was an accomplished axe-man.

I remember the story he used to tell us about the day he noticed my mother. My father had been working at the farm every summer for about two years. It was an extremely hot day in August, the "dog days," as they called it. They were out scything hay by hand. He was dying of thirst. He told us that when he looked up, "I thought I saw an angel and she had a pail of cold water." A young lass came up to the men with a pail of fresh drinking water from the nearby brook, her silhouette standing out against the sky in a field of sweet red clover. He heard a voice saying to him, "That's the girl you're going to marry." The angel with the pail of cold water was Lucinda Francis Boynton, the farmer's daughter.

He told us, "I was kind of shy in those days and it took me three more summers before I dared talk to her."

A Happy Home: Marm's Story

When my mother, Lucinda Boynton, was eight-years old she and her family had to flee from a fire that destroyed much of the town, including their home. Shortly after, her father bought farmland that still needed a lot of land cleared, which is, of course, how my dad came in handy. My grandparents' farm in Stacyville was about a 100 miles north of Bangor and had the best views of the Katahdin Range. It was called the Katahdin Valley Farm. If you were to head due west from Grandfather's farm for 30 or so miles you would never see any signs of civilization, except perhaps for an abandoned logging camp or trapper's cabin. That stretch of woods is probably one of the finest places to hunt deer or catch the sweetest tasting trout.

My grandfather started a logging camp, and he took my mother out of school after her sophomore year to work as a cook. Leaving school kind of broke her heart. She wrote a lot of poetry. She even wrote a memoir. She had a very interesting way of bringing stories alive. She was a great reader too. I can remember as a child how she elaborated on the fairy tales. I think, in a sense, she kind of lived them. She told us many, many of them and she seemed to know them by heart. My mother was a very intelligent person. She would have been way up high if she had the opportunity.

My mother had an older sister, Lota, who was the queen of the ball. According to Lota, my dad didn't have a real job. They considered woodsmen's work a poor job. She would put my mother down an awful lot and she would say, "Don't marry Henry."

Courting in those days was quite different than it is today. You had to be on your best behavior, very polite and considerate. My grandparents trusted my father, though they were strict Baptists. However, there weren't many places you could go. You couldn't just take a girl out on a date. But my mother had a wonderful horse named Maggie and they would go out for rides in the carriage.

Mom did not hesitate to marry Dad, but she placed one condition on him, that he "never go back into the woods camps for the entire

Paul's mother Lucinda Boynton
at 16 years old, 1911

winter again." Smart women knew if you married a woodsman, that probably soon you would become pregnant and have to bear that child alone while your husband was far off in the woods. Dad had to break that promise a few times during the hard years, but never again did he hire out for the entire winter. He was an able carpenter. When there was work, he would tackle any job that would provide him with the necessities his family required.

My mother gave birth to nine babies, all at home: Dorothy Louise is the oldest; next came my brother, Herbert Henry; Ada Mae was born later the same year as Herbert; then came Thelma Ardine, Ruth Winifred, and Robert William; I (Paul Eugene) was born in 1924 in the town of Patten, where we lived till I was eight years old. I was the youngest for a while. Patricia Louise was next, but she died at about three months. I think it was pneumonia. She didn't live very long. Then quite a few years later, after we had moved to Mattawamkeag, my mother, approaching 40, gave birth to my little brother, Richard. He had a cerebral hemorrhage at birth and yet he lived. He was bedridden all his life and Marm took care of him for 27 years. It was not easy. Richard never was able to move at all. She had to feed him. She had to take care of his bowel movements. She had to keep him clean. People would say, "Why don't you put him in a home?"

She'd say, "No, he's my son."

Boynton Family and pulp cutting crew in Crystal, Maine. In the center row (left to right) are my mother Lucinda, my grandmother Nellie, and my grandfather Herbert Boynton wearing hat and suspenders. Seated on the bottom row (left to right) are my father Joseph Henry, longtime family friend Jolie Terrio, and Uncle Bill Boynton. The others are all Polish loggers fresh from Poland. c.1915

I could write a book about my mother. There was a lot of love for my brother. We would have done anything we could have for him.

I remember my family as being a very happy family. People would say, "What do you have to be happy about?" Well, we had each other for one thing and we had a good father and mother. They were naturally good. They really never raised their voices. They never spoke badly of anybody. They were always ready to help people. I never heard them raise their voice at their children or at each other. They never said, "You shouldn't do this." Instead, my mother would very gently say, "We don't do that."

I never heard them complain about the things they had to do. My mother had to raise eight children in rented houses without running water, electricity, central heat or a washing machine. She didn't have a radio or a car or hardly enough clothing of her own, no education beyond her second year of high school, and yet she taught me, quietly, through her way of living, to accept "the cards you were dealt" as the saying goes. She had a lovely voice and I always remember her singing the hymn, "I Need Thee Every Hour." I often have found myself singing those words, and it has helped me through many difficult times.

Marm and Dad's wedding photo, 1914

My first memories are of cold winters, hugging the kitchen cook stove, or crawling in behind the parlor stove, often times falling asleep. Running on my fat little legs to meet Dad as he came home from work, just waiting to be taken upon his shoulders and riding the rest of the way home. That was my favorite place in the entire world.

Patten was my first town, a place that still has a hold on my happiest memories. I can still remember Pleasant Street in Patten in our rented house. We always had to rent, as Dad could never accumulate enough money to build or buy a home of our own. We always called our houses according to who owned them. I was born in the Ethel Mains house. Then we lived in the Richmond House, and the Cunningham House, etc. I really didn't even know that people actually owned their own homes. Dad probably could have borrowed money to build or buy, but he was always too proud to use other people's money. He never owed anyone any money he couldn't pay off with one week's pay.

When I was three years old we moved out of town, north about two miles, where Dad went to work for a man named Charlie Cunningham. Charlie had a pretty good-sized dairy farm and also grew potatoes. Dad was his hired man. We were able to live in a really nice farmhouse owned by Charlie, hence it became known as the Cunningham House, with lots of rooms and a big barn. It was a beautiful place, with a big apple orchard right beside it and a small brook running in back of the house. The house was so warm and snug in the wintertime and cool and breezy in the summer. It was my favorite place. There was a huge attic in the house and that was my playroom. I had it mostly to myself.

I had a dog, Laddie, who just about stepped in every track I made. He was my guardian angel, I guess. I remember going out to the mailbox beside the road to get our mail. In the wintertime I would get stuck in the snow and Laddie would tug and tug at me trying to get me out. When he couldn't do it he ran barking back to the house to get Marm.

When I was still just four years old all of my brothers and sisters were in school. I wanted so badly to go to school with my brothers and sisters. Finally, Marm decided I was ready to go to school, and she took me down when I turned four and enrolled me in the first grade. (There was no kindergarten back then.) I was in seventh heaven. Marm hadn't told the teacher how old I was and the teacher never asked. Two weeks later the teacher sent home a note with one of my sisters. When I happily arrived at home Marm said she had something to tell me. When she revealed what was in the note, tears came into her eyes, but more came into mine. I had to wait to go to school for another year. I was broken hearted.

Marm could always find a way to make an unhappy time become a happy one. She told me she would take care of that problem. She rigged up a school chair and found a broken-down desk for me. Just as soon as I had done my chores after breakfast she started teaching me. I spent hours at that desk doing all kinds of "school work." The next September I was allowed to enter the first grade. The teacher was surprised to see how much I already knew.

To Mattawamkeag

My father could never afford to buy a house. In the little northern Maine town of Patten we moved from one house to another, always renting. In 1932, when I was in third grade, Dad got a job operating a sawmill, and so we moved to another little northern Maine town, Mattawamkeag, just one week before Christmas.

We had no means of transportation, but Henry Olsen, Dad's operating companion, offered to move our family in his car. Mr. Olsen's car couldn't carry all of us; for the first trip it was only Marm and four of us kids. Mr. Olsen had worked that day and came all the way from Mattawamkeag just to get us. We loaded up and headed for Mattawamkeag 45 miles away, only a few hours before dark. It seemed like moving across the country. We had never ventured far from Patten before, except by horse and wagon.

All seemed well in that first hour, but as quite often happens in December in Maine, it began to snow. It came lightly at first, but within a short time it was coming down quite heavily. Halfway from Patten to Mattawamkeag there is a rather mean stretch of woods knows as the Nine Mile Woods. I had heard much of this mysterious place, how cars break down there, that there are no houses or accommodations along that stretch. When someone breaks down, they are stuck there. Just hearing about it gave me a creepy feeling.

By the time we entered that spooky stretch it had snowed over 12 inches already. A snowplow had preceded us, but the road was still snowy and icy. I worried we would get stuck in the Nine Mile Woods. Marm knew we were concerned and started singing Christmas carols, and we all joined in. That took our minds off the scary possibilities. We started going down a long steep hill very, very cautiously. As we inched along we began to see lights far down the hill. Almost immediately my mind went far off to "The Little Town of Bethlehem," and I started singing. I just knew if we were going to Bethlehem soon we would be all right.

As we crept closer into the town we saw more and more streetlights and even lights inside houses. I wondered which one might be our new home. Mattawamkeag is not a very big town and soon we passed by most of the houses. I began to feel a little bit concerned. We passed by fewer and fewer lights and houses, and then we turned off the main road and onto an unplowed road. It was dark, really dark. We stopped singing Christmas carols.

Mr. Olsen slowly came to a stop. By then it was quite late, but we could see a rather dim light coming from a window. It looked more like a horse stable than a house. The four of us kids didn't say a word or make a sound. A door opened. A man stepped out carrying a lantern and came right up to the car. It was Dad!

Our Tarpaper Shack

Our new home in Mattawamkeag was what was known as a tarpaper shack, quite a common type of housing during the Great Depression. It was 14 feet by 20 feet the size of a single-car garage. Dad built it on a piece of land that he paid $8 a month to rent. It was a shed-like building constructed of rough-sawn pine, two by four studs and rafters, one door, and four windows. The roof was covered with cedar shingles. The exterior was covered with tarpaper, which was black but could easily be whitewashed. It was not insulated as we think of today, but the inside walls were also covered with tarpaper. There was a stove in the middle for warmth and cooking. We roasted in the summers but were as warm as toast in the winters.

Dad built bunk beds along the walls, double ones so that two or three kids could bunk in one of them, which gave plenty of sleeping space for all seven of us. The four girls slept in the first two double bunks, and Herbie had his own bunk on the other side. Bob and I slept in the other double bunk. Dad made a bed with a straw mattress for him and Marm. We had no furniture, but Dad built some pine slab makeshift cupboards at one end and a makeshift table near the other end. We had a henhouse and a pigpen. There was a "backhouse," also referred to as a "three-holer." The holes were shaped to fit the varying sizes of the members of the family. I will leave that term to your imagination.

We moved a week before Christmas and cut our own Christmas tree shortly after our arrival, which we decorated with pinecones, popcorn balls and anything we could conjure up to make it look bright. That was how we spent Christmas of 1932 and many more after that. "Camp" was our place of abode for the next seven years. Those were some of the happiest days in my memory.

Life began anew in this very different town. Although population-wise, it was even smaller than Patten. We lived about a mile and a half from town, and the only way to get there was to walk. We followed an unused road through the woods, which we named Crooked Street. It really was just used by trucks to gain access to a near-by gravel pit. The road was so crooked the trucks had to meander around some very large pine trees. It was never plowed in the wintertime, but all seven of us kids used it. Usually the older ones made a good path for me to follow. No one besides us ever walked it because of all the mud puddles in the spring after a rain. However, I found great joy in those mud puddles. I built dams and canals and floated my little boats that I made out of paper I took home from the wastebaskets at school.

The summer after we moved into our camp Dad carried home free pine slabs from the mill and soon constructed a shed-like structure attached to the end of the camp for a kitchen. He cut a door in the back of the camp, which gave us entrance to this shed. When he finished it, Uncle Leo arrived from the farm in Patten in his truck with our good old Round Oak cooking stove, a monstrosity. That humungous hunk of metal could eat up wood faster than a kid can eat up half a dozen cookies. The top was three feet by six feet with six cooking holes. The two ovens under the cooktop could easily hold a full meal of chicken, two-dozen biscuits, a dozen or more baking potatoes, and a family-sized pan of cornbread. On the top of the stove was a shelf with doors that could hold all the hot food until it was ready to be served at the family table.

The stove also featured an attached 10-gallon water tank so we could have hot water. The tank had to be filled by someone, and I soon learned that I was that someone along with my brother, Bob.

Dad dug out a spring in the woods, about 100 yards or so away from the camp. That spring supplied us with all the water we needed. I usually had to fill the tank twice a day. In the summer it was kind of fun, but when the snow got to be two and three feet deep, all the fun was gone. I could only carry one 10-quart pail at a time, and the tank took about four or five pails. How well I remember carrying a pail in the deep snow with the water slopping over and filling my rubber boots.

Saturday was the toughest time, because Marm, who was a stickler for cleanliness, did her washing on that day and we all had our weekly baths. Just imagine how much water it would take for nine people to take a bath, though we didn't change the water every time. It seems like I carried water all day long. In the winter, I had to carry a hatchet with me to chop away the ice to get a pail into the spring.

I once had the great idea to hitch up my German shepherd, Poddy, and that would be the end of my pail-carrying days. I made a harness for him and Dad got a set of small bobsleds from somewhere. Well, Poddy loved the sled, but somehow when he had two pails of water on the sled, he wanted to run, and soon the pails were empty. So, my dream of a mechanized water supply was gone.

We always had all of the wood needed to keep us warm. We cut our own firewood nearby in the big woods, usually about five cords for a year. We used a bucksaw, a crosscut saw, and an ax. Dad had to pay "stumpage" for the wood, meaning he had to give the woods owner one cord for each cord of wood he cut for himself. We had to haul it all ourselves on a small "moose sled," which was normally used to haul a dead moose out of the woods. The moose sleds were about ten feet long, a couple of feet wide with boards to lay the moose on, and all connected to two curved boards used as runners. Of course, fancy mill-made sleds had metal runners. One or two people pulled it over the snow with leather straps.

Marshall family home from 1932 to 1939, Mattawamkeag, Maine

Another wonderful surprise was when Uncle Leo brought our big old oak table. That was Marm and Dad's first purchase when they got married. It had four leaves that you insert to make the table bigger so that all nine of us, plus one visitor could sit at the table for a meal. In the new shed, which we called the "kitchen," there was room enough for our Round Oak stove and our round table, as well as some new pine slab shelves for Marm, and lest I forget, the huge wood box. Guess who got the opportunity to keep that filled? Right! Yours truly. My brother Bob somehow seemed to always be busy playing sports, so I had the blessing of filling the wood box. Somehow, I never minded those chores and I always had a good feeling when I had accomplished them. Plus, it meant that Marm had enough wood to bake yeast bread every Saturday, and we always had a good supply of Saturday baked beans, usually enough to last us all week.

The Great Depression did not seem to have much of a grip on my family. We heard about people who were starving and sick with nowhere to live. We lived simply, but we survived. In the winter we had a nice warm tarpaper shack to live in and in the summer, we lived in tents. We had all we wanted to eat and wear, and never had any sickness other than the usual maladies and occasional stomach aches from eating too much of Marm's excellent cooking. We were happy!

We had a cow named Mary who was more like a member of the family than just another animal. When Dad got off work at the sawmill, the end of the workday was signaled with a loud whistle from the engine letting off steam. As soon as Mary heard the mill whistle blow, she would start bellowing and keep it up until Dad got home and milked her.

Mary gave us over ten quarts of milk in the morning and again at night, so we had all of the milk and cream we wanted. She also supplied good fertilizer for our garden.

We also had laying hens, enough to give us all the eggs we needed and a chicken dinner every Sunday. We always had two or three pigs that grew and grew and grew during the summer. Come late fall, they became pork, lard, bacon, and all that. We didn't even have to buy feed, as there was plenty right around us in the open fields and in the woods.

Dad was a genius about gardening. We had all we could eat during the summer and Marm would can string beans, corn, beets, pickled cucumber, tomatoes, and all sorts of greens, enough to last us all winter. I'll bet you are wondering where we stored all of those canned goods. Well, let me explain.

The first summer in Mattawamkeag Dad began digging a cave into a gravel bank near the camp on the edge of the woods. Every night when he came home from the mill he would side track over to the railroad yard and carry an old discarded cedar railroad tie home with him, quite a muscular feat. Soon he was stacking those ties one on top of the other, constructing the three sides of a structure, eight feet high. He carried more railroad ties to put a flat roof across the walls. He covered the structure with gravel and made a solid, double-thick door out of pine slabs. That was our root cellar, where we kept all of Marm's preserves and root vegetables like potatoes, carrots, beets, turnips and such.

Even on a cold stormy winter's day we could plod our way out to the root cellar and bring home enough food for a couple of days. In the fall there was still enough space left to hang up a good size deer. In the hot summer, it served as a cooler where we kept many quarts of

Paul Marshall, 1933

homemade root beer and stored our daily milk supply. We never had a refrigerator or even an icebox like some homes had in those days.

We also snared rabbits and Marm could make the best pies you ever saw out of what we caught in those snares. The nearby Mattawamkeag River abounded with smallmouth bass, eels, and occasionally pickerel, so we had plenty of fish. In the summer, a couple of brooks back in the woods usually gave a few special meals of brook trout.

I spent early summer digging dandelion greens that I could sell for 15 cents a peck to town folks. When the raspberry and blackberry season came around, I could pick and sell berries for 10 cents a quart. That gave me lots of money to buy fish hooks and sinkers for fishing.

Marm was a fantastic cook and could make a delicious meal out of anything. We always had delicious pies, cakes, cookies, and home-made bread. We had lots of seasonal strawberries, raspberries, blackberries, and dandelions that were free for the picking, and they were always plentiful if one had the gumption to get out and get them. Marm's raspberry bakersheet pies couldn't be beat.

Every one of my mother's meals was just absolutely wonderful. She often cooked deer meat. We didn't have fancy kinds of foods, just common foods. Even still my favorite meal is meat, potatoes, and vegetables. My mother used to make creamed carrots. She cooked them and then mashed them with a potato masher and then added cream and butter. Saturday was bread and baked beans day. The whole house smelled for yards around. There was always hot biscuits and hot bread.

We never bought store bread; we never had the money for it. People used to say, "Wow, your mother is a wonderful cook."

Let me tell you about our lunch pails. As we were a fairly good-sized family—seven of us children and not too easily fed, one of our favorite lunches was a simple sandwich with peanut butter and one of Marm's special jams: strawberry, blackberry, raspberry, blueberry, and sometimes even gooseberry. We had lots of all of those because they grew wild within just a few 100 feet from our camp. The peanut butter came in two-quart pails. Once the pails were empty, we turned them into lunch pails for all seven of us and for Dad as well. The pails also made perfect containers for picking berries.

I know it must seem to those who read this that all I thought of was food. Well, I guess that is true. With such a big family to feed, and only one person working for money, everyone had to think a lot about food and how to get it.

The Maine Woods

My early memories are of running on my fat little legs to meet Dad as he came home from work, just waiting to be taken upon his shoulders and riding the rest of the way home. That was my favorite place in the entire world. How often he would take me on his shoulders and we would walk in the woods, me riding high and blowing on one of his willow whistles, which seemed to appear magically from his razor-sharp jackknife.

I loved to play in the pile of shavings that came from his jackknife and his "crooked knife" as he whittled and shaved out perfect axe handles from the perfect straightness of the ash bolts. He always finished his handles into complete smoothness with broken pieces of glass he saved just for this purpose. Many times I would go into the woods with him on a Sunday morning and watch him make his choice of just the right ash sapling to cut and make the bolts for his handles, rejecting this tree and that one, for their defects, and finally settling on one that God must have grown just for axe handles.

Dad never talked much and was always very quiet on our walks in the woods; sometimes he whistled a little tune, but very quietly. Then he would stop and just stand still. I would soon see why. There in a branch, a slight movement, and then…a LOUD flutter, and a partridge flew up, the sound jumping the daylights out of me, as the bird made its hasty retreat. Somehow, my dad just knew that bird was in there. I guess you get that way living among the creatures of the big woods. A partridge, or as they say in Maine *pat-ridge*, was often the best meal for a hungry woodsman. At other times, Dad would just point his finger very slowly, and when my eyes followed the direction of his finger, sure enough, there in the *pucker brush* (a Mainer word for dense undergrowth) could be seen a beautiful doe and usually hidden nearby stood her lamb.

The woods, which stretched for probably at least a 100 miles in practically every direction, became my playground. I was never afraid to go off alone and simply explore. I learned to walk softly like my dad. I heard of how Native Americans can sneak up so silently on a deer, close enough to shoot it with an arrow, killing it instantly. Also, my summer shoes (we only had one pair of summer shoes and one pair of winter boots) in those days were leather moccasins, the old kind without soles, and wearing those you could very easily sneak along quite silently.

Much of my boyhood was spent simply wandering off into the woods. It seemed a challenge to go out and see if I could find my way back. My dog, Poddy (short for Partner), was always right at my heels, except when he would sneak off after a rabbit. But he always came back sooner or later, so I never felt alone. My goal often was to sneak up, Indian-style on some unaware creature, even if it was just a *pat-ridge*, but hopefully it would be a deer. In doing that sometimes I would lose track of where I was and then I would have to determine which way to go to get back home. Of course, it never occurred to me that Poddy would have no trouble leading me back home if need be.

I loved the woods, how they changed from low, swampy ground with beautifully smelling white cedar, to balsam fir, and white and red

Wassataquoik Stream, a favorite fishing stream for the Marshalls, 1948

spruce, to the huge white pines and paper birches and beeches hanging with delicious beechnuts, and so on, up to the higher ground. I used the lay of the land as my guide to where I was going, so I could easily find my way back home. I often ventured alone considerable distances from home. I loved to follow a brook. If you travel alone in the deep woods where there are no sounds except the natural ones, you can hear a brook long before you can see it. I could write a book about brooks. One of my favorite poems is "The Brook" by Alfred Lord Tennyson. I loved it when I first heard it read to me by Marm, and it was the first one I learned by heart at school.

> I come from haunts of coot and hern,
> I make a sudden sally,
> And sparkle out among the fern,
> To bicker down a valley.
>
> By thirty hills I hurry down,
> Or slip between the ridges,

By twenty thorps, a little town,
And half a hundred bridges.

Till last by Philip's farm I flow
To join the brimming river,
For men may come and men may go,
But I go on forever.

I chatter over stony ways,
In little sharps and trebles,
I bubble into eddying bays,
I babble on the pebbles.

With many a curve my banks I fret
by many a field and fallow,
And many a fairy foreland set
With willow-weed and mallow.

I chatter, chatter, as I flow
To join the brimming river,
For men may come and men may go,
But I go on forever.

I wind about, and in and out,
with here a blossom sailing,
And here and there a lusty trout,
And here and there a grayling,

And here and there a foamy flake
Upon me, as I travel
With many a silver water-break
Above the golden gravel,

And draw them all along, and flow
To join the brimming river,
For men may come and men may go,
But I go on forever.

I steal by lawns and grassy plots,
I slide by hazel covers;
I move the sweet forget-me-nots
That grow for happy lovers.

I slip, I slide, I gloom, I glance,
Among my skimming swallows;
I make the netted sunbeam dance
Against my sandy shallows.

I murmur under moon and stars
In brambly wildernesses;
I linger by my shingly bars;
I loiter round my cresses;

And out again I curve and flow
To join the brimming river,
For men may come and men may go,
But I go on forever.

      I loved and lived that poem. I could follow a brook forever, always wondering what was just around the next bend. I believe, in a sense, it became the basis for my life.

      The Maine woods are like a history book to me. They begin as an un-named, un-obstructed phenomenon, no roads, only footpaths and deer trails. Horses and oxen began to change the woods. Clearings were made to grow hay to feed those powerful work animals. Those horses and oxen were essential for hauling logs, wagons, and sleds carrying supplies far back into the depths of the forest. Then came the first engines to go deep into the Maine woods, "log haulers," they were called, huge steam vehicles that could handle just about any type of forest in any season with their broad caterpillar treads. They made in-roads into the Maine forests deeper and deeper. Those steam monsters could haul as many as 20 and 30 log-loaded sleds from the cutting grounds miles to local sawmills and later to the railroad stations. Those log roads had been active for many years when gasoline engines began taking the place of the steam engines and the road had to be upgraded so that rubber-tired trucks could do the hauling. And now, new machinery, bulldozers, tree cutters and trimmers that can be operated by a single man, are the monsters eating up the forest and going deeper and deeper into the heartland. But all of this is history, and history is still in the making.

One of the many pleasures of living in northern Maine is the freedom to step out of your back door with your rifle or your shotgun in your hand and wander the woods in search of a good hunt. Hunting was a way of life back then. Our camp was right on the edge of the big woods, and deer liked to come out to feed along the fields at the edge of the woods. They even liked our gardens. We had deer meat all year round. I don't know whether Dad had a hunting license or not, or even whether one was required, but during the Depression, game wardens didn't bother with large families like ours because they knew we had to have meat to keep us healthy. They were too busy chasing down poachers. (Those were guys who shot lots of deer and sold them to the "sportsmen from away" who came to Maine to get their trophy deer, even if they didn't shoot it themselves.)

The goal of the backwoods hunter was to bring home meat for the dinner table. Hunting was not a sport as it is nowadays; it was a way of living. Large families had to have food, so hunting deer, moose, bear, rabbits, and such was a good source of food for our family. A boy in northern Maine just naturally became a hunter.

There are two distinct ways to hunt deer. One way to hunt is to take what they call a "stand" along a deer path or in a place where deer go for food or water, and just wait for the deer to come. The other way is to locate some fresh tracks and follow them, sneaking very quietly along until you come upon a deer. This works fine especially if there is any amount of snow on the ground. Tracking is much more exciting and takes a good deal more skill than just sitting and waiting until the deer come to you, but it means that the hunter may travel a goodly distance, and not even catch up with a deer. Also, you may get a bit lost and confused since your mind is on the deer and not where you have traveled.

There is a story about Daniel Boone, the great wilderness explorer. Someone once asked Daniel if he ever got lost, and Daniel's reply was: "Well, no. I was a bit bewildered for about three months, but I wasn't ever lost." That's how I sometimes felt when I went some distance away from home. I got to know the hills and the bogs and the brooks and the in-between land and could always get back home one way or another.

When I reached the age of 12, I was allowed to carry a gun and search for deer, birds, or rabbits—all of which meant a good meal back home. I admit I didn't have a license at that time. I only had a bird gun, a 20-gauge shotgun that mostly was good for killing birds and even rabbits; the chances of killing a deer were pretty slim.

Sometimes I went out hoping to scare up a partridge. Though the phrase *scare up* should really refer to the hunter who generally is the one who gets "scared up." Partridges seem to have uniquely sensitive hearing and will let you get very close, and then when it is deadly silent, the bird will take off as fast and loud as a fighter jet. Many times while hunting I have nearly taken off myself when the bird zoomed up only a few feet away. Of course the goal of a good hunter is to get at least one shot at the zooming bird and bring home a delicious "woods chicken" supper. Quite often that was my pleasure.

Deer have a very keen sense of smell, so if you want to sneak up on one you have to be downwind of the deer, because it can easily smell you when you are upwind even a half a mile or so away.

The first time I shot a deer I snuck up on a couple feeding in a swamp. I got close enough to try to shoot one. I picked the smallest one because I knew that my 20-gauge might not do much harm to a big one. I hit that little one and he went down, but he wasn't dead. He just cried the blats out of him, and it made me feel awful. I knew there was only one thing for me to do, and that was to get as close as I could to him and let him have it right in the head to put him out of his misery. I tell you, that was one of the most distressful days of my life. I wasn't very proud of myself.

Early on, I found it was not the thrill of killing an animal, but the thrill of being out there in the woods and exploring that I enjoyed so much. There was just so much out there to see that I hadn't seen before.

I also became an avid trout fisherman and fished many of the streams of northern Maine. Perhaps my greatest joy was to pack an overnight pack, stick out my thumb to get a ride, get dropped off near some stream and then follow that stream for a day or two. When I had enough of fishing I would locate the nearest road and could easily find my way home. I seemed to have a natural sense of direction and mostly enjoyed following a stream, just to see what was around the next bend.

Growing up on the edge of the vast Maine woods, especially during the Depression, was an experience in survival. Yet, our kind of living taught us the true values in life. I feel these experiences helped to shape my future more than any others that I can recall.

The Great Depression

We didn't know anything about the Depression. The newspapers didn't say much about it. Nobody had a radio. Sometimes we had enough money to go to the movies; matinees cost only 10 cents back then. Before the show they'd play a newsreel showing the bread lines in New York and things like that. That was all we knew about the Depression. I used to think those people were depressed. We didn't know much about it in the Maine woods because we always had plenty to eat: deer meat, rabbits, *pat-ridges*, lots of trout and other fish caught in the nearby brooks and streams. In the summertime we had plenty of wild strawberries, raspberries, blackberries, and garden stuff.

We didn't have an unemployment problem in northern Maine either. Men could always find work if they weren't too fussy. I never knew anybody in town who was out of work. There were mills and woods work. You could clean and cut pulp. You could work on the road. Everything was done by hand and the Depression never touched our town. We didn't know anything about it. My dad said he would do anything for work. He was a woodsman and a rough-carpenter. He could always find some way to bring home enough money to keep the family going. On weekends he cleaned out people's backhouses.

Even as kids we had ways of making money. My older brothers and sisters worked summers at the local match mill, as maids for the motor camps along the highways, and waiting tables at the local restaurant.

There was an old man in town that used coal to heat his house. Another kid and I would go to the railroads and pick up coal that had fallen off the trains and onto the tracks. We'd get 5 cents for a ten-quart bucket of coal. Sometimes we couldn't find any coal, so we'd throw snowballs at the workers. They would see us with our pails and they knew what we were doing so they'd throw coal back at us. It was a game. All the engineers did it.

I used to pick wild raspberries, strawberries, and blackberries and sell them for 25 cents a peck. That seemed like a lot of money. For a peck of dandelion greens I could get 15 cents. When I got to be nine years old I began to mow lawns around town. For a medium-sized lawn I charged 25 cents and for a large one I got 35 cents. Those "self-propelled" lawn mowers didn't propel themselves. You did it yourself, and they were sometimes a bit of a struggle.

When I was ten years old I was able to pick potatoes in the fall. In northern Maine when the potatoes were ripe school closed for two weeks and nearly all the kids were hired to pick potatoes. That job consisted of following a horse-drawn digger and picking on your hands and knees as fast as you could. The digging began as early in the morning as the weather permitted, but usually there was frost all over the ground since it was in October, which made potato-picking a miserably cold adventure. I carried a bushel-sized basket, and when that was full I dumped it into a large wooden barrel. My first potato picking paid me 8 cents for a barrel and my first day out I picked ten barrels, a total income of 80 cents. Later on I could fill up around 40 to 50 barrels.

All that money went to buy my winter clothes, usually a pair of gum-rubber boots, a jacket, maybe a shirt and a pair of pants, and of course long underwear (a dire necessity winters in northern Maine). I really never had to worry much about my clothes as I was the youngest in the family and I got all those clothes my older siblings grew out of. I remember feeling pretty big when I could wear my oldest brother's jackets.

Occasionally men riding the rails showed up in Mattawamkeag. Some were looking for work; those we called *hobos*. But others were simply traveling free and seeking free food, and those were referred to as *bums*. Most of us kids played around the railroad station and very often we would meet up with a hobo. They were always asking for food so I would tell them to come to my house and my mother would give them food because she was such a good cook. The first couple of times I tried that Marm was a bit put out with me, but she also had a feeling for those unfortunate men and would gladly give them something to eat.

Doctor Carl Trout Saves the Day

One day a new doctor, Dr. Carl Trout, set-up his office in town and put up his sign. There was just one hitch. It didn't say, *Dr. Carl Trout, M.D.* as in a medical doctor, instead his name was followed by *D.O.* as in a doctor of osteopathic medicine. Most people in town had never heard of such a thing as osteopathy. What was it, and what did he do? People were saying, "Well, he isn't a *real* doctor."

It wasn't long before people began calling him for their medical needs. Babies were being born and people were coming down with colds and flu and such, and they needed a doctor. He made house calls all over town and in nearby towns, to camps and farmhouses. Dr. Trout went out to logging camps and checked on the men now and then. Dr. Trout helped a lot of people, but I particularly remember how he helped my dad.

Dad was working in the sawmill and a huge pine log rolled off a truck and broke both of his legs. The men went as fast as they could to find Dr. Trout, and luckily he was in is office. He jumped in his car and drove to the mill. The men lifted Dad into the back seat. The doctor brought him to our home only to tell Marm that he was planning to drive him to get x-rays in Lincoln, 12 miles away.

Marm couldn't leave all my brothers and sisters alone, so she told me to go along with the Doctor and Dad. I was 12 years old. I rode in the back seat with Dad trying to comfort him. He was in bad pain even though Dr. Trout had given him some painkillers. When we got to the hospital in Lincoln we found that their x-ray machine was down, and the nearest one was 50 miles away in Bangor. Dr. Trout said, "Go home and tell your mother." We had no telephone at home so it was the only way she would know what was happening.

Twelve miles away from home I started running. When cars came by, I stuck out my thumb, but nobody would pick me up. After I ran four or five miles. I started crying because I had the feeling I might not see Dad again. Then, finally a car stopped and it just happened to be my next-door neighbor. He took me home and I told Marm what happened. She took it very quietly, as was her usual way. We all felt so helpless.

Four hours later Dr. Trout pulled into the yard. We weren't sure we wanted to hear what he would say. But his first words were, "Don't worry, everything will be all right. He must stay in the hospital for a few days, but I will go down and get him when he's ready." Three days later Dr. Trout brought Dad home to us.

I've Been Working on the Railroad

As a kid I was often late for school because I had to cross the rail yard on my way there and I liked to stop at the train station. In Mattawamkeag railroads were like blood vessels for the town. They brought life to the town, excitement, and employment for men of all ages. The Canadian Pacific Railroad ran through our town from Halifax all the way to Montreal, so there were always trains coming and going. Inside the station, I would get warm by the nice fire from the pot-bellied stove. It definitely was a good place when the temperature was down below zero, which was often the case. I remember the huge steam locomotives, huffing and puffing as though they were out of breath. Before they'd head out of the station they'd blow their whistle and puff even more, and the engineers always waved at me. As I stood there watching them go, I often wished someday I could be a railroad engineer.

By 1939 my older brothers and sisters were trying to earn money to pay for their college expenses, and they had already gone off to their summer jobs. My dad was still recovering from his injury. He tried to work on crutches, but it was just about impossible to do woods work, and so we were left with no income at that time. I thought if we were able to bring home any money at all it would surely be a blessing. I was determined to do what I could to help.

The railroads always needed "extra gang" workers during the summer to help lay new track. I knew the work would be extremely difficult, but I was in pretty good shape at 16. The legal age to work for the railroad was 18, but the railroad boss never asked for birth certificates. If you looked like you could sling a ten-pound sledgehammer for ten hours a day he'd hire you because they needed men. But he expected everyone to do as much as the other members of the gang. I was hired and felt pretty proud. I could hardly wait to tell Marm and Dad. They didn't want me to go, but they never stood in the way of any of us children.

The work site was 55 miles from my home in Mattawamkeag. We left on a Sunday night on the eight o'clock passenger train and sat on the floor of the caboose next to the conductor. When the train came to a stop in the middle of nowhere the conductor yelled at us, "Get off this train. We've got a schedule to keep!" We were left standing on the side of the tracks in the dark waiting for someone to tell us where to go. Soon a guy with a lantern came along and led us over to several old passenger cars. We were told these would be our living quarters. When we went inside we could see by the lantern-light that there were lots of beds. Upon closer examination, we discovered the beds were actually passenger seats that had been lowered so that they formed a bed with room enough for two or even three sleepers if necessary.

The car filled up fast and I was left along with some others without a bed. So the boss led us out to a boxcar, which is really just a huge crate with wide open doors on each side. It was near midnight and we were glad to find a place to sleep inside. Without a lantern it was a bit difficult to see what was in the car but four of us did find a place to lie down. There was no bedding but we had been told to bring along a blanket with us, and it was not very long before we were all sleeping.

At six o'clock the boss's aide walked through the car and yelled, "Board!" which meant, get out of bed, get dressed, and head for the dining car. No chance for a wash-up or relieving ourselves (which we had to do in the woods). By then there was sufficient sunlight to see inside our boxcar. We looked around and saw many small wooden boxes stacked up along the walls, labeled in huge letters, TNT. We had been sleeping in the explosives car! And here I'd been smoking a cigarette before going to sleep last night! I thought briefly of quitting smoking when I read that sign. That sleeping arrangement was mine for the rest of the summer.

Our crew consisted of around 40 men, all of whom had to be fed right there on the job. An old passenger car was our dining room, except that there were no seats, only two long tables arranged for standing room while eating. I am still amazed when I think of the quantity and the content of each meal, even the breakfast. I had never seen so much food all at one time, but you had to eat as fast as you could because you would be slinging the hammer by seven o'clock. The next time we heard *board* it meant go to work.

Transportation to the worksite was by "pump car," a four-wheeled flat car that was propelled by moving an apparatus with handles in the middle of the car. Four men pumped the handles up and down to make the wheels turn and the car move forward. There was no reverse. If you wanted to go the other way, all the riders had to get off, lift the entire car, turn it around, and then go on their way. It was somewhat over-loaded, but 10 men could ride on one pump car. There were at least four cars in action for the 40-man crew. Each crew had to lift the car to get it set on the tracks. If we heard the whistle of a train far off, we had to get the pump car off the track as swiftly as possible and clear off before that monster came puffing along trying to keep on schedule. There were times when that whistle seemed mighty close and those heavy cars were just about all 10 men could manage to lift.

At the site, the boss looked us over quickly and immediately decided which assignment would best fit each of us. When he looked at me he saw a 5-foot, 5-inch boy who probably weighed no more that 140 pounds. He probably thought I wouldn't be able to last very long slinging a 10-pound sledgehammer 10 hours a day. He assigned me to be a "tamper," a job that involved moving a spade along the edge of the ties and pushing gravel under and around it. I really had hoped that I would be a "hammer man," driving the spikes that held the rails in place, so I asked if I could do that instead. The boss simply laughed out loud, but then he looked at me for a minute and said, "You asked for it, you're going to get it!" I wasn't quite sure as to just what he meant by that, but I soon learned his meaning.

My first day on the hammer felt like it would be my last day on the job. We were not supplied with any gloves and my soft hands soon began to blister. I tried tying rags to my hands and that helped a bit. Of course we didn't have any fancy bandage stuff, but later my mother gave me an old sheet that I carried with me just for that purpose.

We worked from six in the morning until six in the evening, with occasional breaks for a snack or a drink of water, which was carried by a young kid, sometimes for over half a mile from a brook. The work was extremely hard, but the food was great. That summer we replaced

25 miles of track from Greenville to Jackman. We tore out all of the old railroad ties and rails and replaced them.

Once the ties were tamped in, a 32-foot, 800-pound solid piece of steel had to be picked up and carried onto its position on the ties. The steel rails were dropped off alongside the working area so that our men had to carry them a short distance and place them in the right position on the ties. Usually 8 men carried a rail into position with tongs, but there were times when 4 men had to do the job. That meant carrying nearly 200 pounds per man. There was no easy work in laying steel.

Next, 100-pound wooden kegs were rolled off the flat cars. The kegs had a mind of their own and many of them kept right on rolling and ended up 100 feet or more down the steep bank of the new bed. Trying to get a 100-pound keg up a steep gravel bank was another trick, but it had to be done.

Once two rails were in place they were joined together by a metal coupling and then fastened to the ties with four 6-inch steel spikes, and that's where the hammer men came in. Next, somebody else came along attaching nuts and bolts to each side of the couplings. Without a doubt, the easiest task was tightening up the final bolts. All the "nut-man" had to do was wait until everything was done and then he could do his work.

Hammer men had a bit of a rest time, a matter of a few minutes, between the laying and tamping of new ties and the laying of the rail and the couplings. I would look at my hands and wonder, "Can I stay with it?" The blisters, plus the June temperatures in Maine, can very soon take the "big man" feeling right out of you, but I couldn't quit! Besides, I couldn't get home until Saturday. Five o'clock seemed like eternity. Break time came at ten o'clock. Snacks and cold water helped a bit. No one talked about how hard the work was. No one shirked on the job. A half hour at noontime was like a dream. Back to work.

One way to get a half-hour of rest for a hammer man was to pretend you missed the spike accidentally. It wasn't too difficult for a good hammerer when he was driving spikes to miss the spike on purpose, and the purpose behind that act was to get a break on a real steaming hot day. If the hammer head missed the spike the handle would come across the rail in such a manner that it immediately snapped, thus putting the hammer out of action. If your hammer handle broke it was your responsibility to re-hang a new handle, which took about a half-hour and that half hour was a pretty good break-time. The boss was aware of this, but if it didn't occur too often with the same hammerer, he would let it pass. It didn't take very much goofing off to get fired, and that just wasn't in the book of a good worker. Dishonesty in Maine was not looked upon very friendly like.

At five o'clock we'd get a signal from the boss. That's it. Throw the pump wagons onto the track. Pump our way back home to our sleeping car.

"Hey, there's a stream." Just time to jump in and get cleaned up. Of course none of us had any soap.

"Hey. There's some dish soap in the kitchen. No, you don't need a towel." Just as well. None of us had one.

"Supper!!!!" And you could eat as much as you wanted.

Yes, I was tired. Yes, I was ready to quit. Yes, I ached all over. I looked at my hands and wondered if I could last one more day. Eventually, someone showed up with some sort of salve or ointment to use on our hands. It did ease up the blisters, which by this time had pretty well broken. Some kind of stuff they called *toilet paper*, a rough brownish stuff that could have been used to card down a horse, showed up, and we used it to wrap up our hands. It eased the pain somewhat and took care of the bleeding. I grabbed several big pieces and stuffed them away for tomorrow to wrap around my hands, although it felt like sandpaper.

There wasn't much sociability there on the siding. Some of the guys took short walks after supper. A few tried fishing in the brook, but most of us went to our beds and some even immediately fell asleep. Those were the days of comic books, which were plentiful in the extra gang. They got passed and passed around until there was nothing left but shreds. I hasten to say that they might have also served as toilet paper, somewhat better than the sandpaper type.

There is one recollection of my days on the line I would like to forget. About half way through the summer we got a new machine called a madding machine. It had a crane arm that would swing out and pick up a section of rail with tongs and place it on the next set of pre-laid ties. That action saved four to eight men having to carry the 32-foot rail, which weighed over 800 pounds. That new machine was certainly a muscle saver, but it could be dangerous too.

One day we were getting ready to lay another rail in place and the chain on the crank slipped. The entire rail crashed to the ground and the crank handle spun around out of control. The handle hit a man standing nearby lifting him far off the ground and dropping him back down. We loaded a pump car on the rails as fast as possible and placed his injured body onto it. Four of us, plus the injured man headed off for the hospital in Greenville, 15 miles away.

I don't think I ever strained as hard as I did that morning. Of course we had no radio to let anyone know we were coming. Fortunately there were no freight trains coming or going at that particular time. Though I doubt we would have stopped even if there had been a train coming at us. We were determined to get our man to the hospital. We didn't stop pumping until we got to the station in Greenville. The station-master got on the phone and called an ambulance to the site. Our boy was still unconscious, but I was amazed that he was still alive.

The happiest day with the extra gang was Saturday. We still worked on Saturday mornings, but mostly just repaired our tools and cleaned up the general area. At noon we lined up before the boss, who was seated at a makeshift table outside of the sleeper cars. This was payday! When your name was called you stepped up to that table to receive your pay, 12 silver dollars! I had never held so much money in my hands before. It seemed to weigh a ton in my pocket but I couldn't keep my hands off it. I must have held it in my hands all the way to Mattawamkeag when I went back home.

Exactly at one o'clock we heard the welcoming whistle of the freight train that would transport us back to Mattawamkeag for a short visit home. We wore the only clothes we had come with. All 40 of us boarded the train, sitting or standing in any place we could find a safe place to ride. Occasionally there would be an empty boxcar that some would jump into, others even got into the caboose. I always enjoyed riding in the engine and sitting on the coal bin. Though they kept shoveling coal into the firebox and my seat kept moving. I had to keep watch that cinders from the engine didn't catch on my clothes or hair. The scenery was beautiful and there was something about being that close to the engineer that I really liked.

I think my greatest joy of all of those summers was after our three-hour ride; I hopped off the train and ran along the track lines for about a mile till I reached home. Those 12 silver dollars seemed awful heavy in my overall pocket but it didn't slow me down. At home Dad would be sitting in his chair, his crutches by his side. I couldn't wait to get ten of those 12 silver dollars out of my pocket and place them in his hand. I can still see the tears in his eyes as he just sat there and let them run.

Then I always took a short run to the river and jumped right in with all my clothes on to wash off all of the railroad dirt that had accumulated during the week. I had very little time before I had to dress up, grab my trumpet, and head for the grange hall for the weekly Saturday night dance.

The Agitators

Church and the Victrola were my first introductions to the world of music, but there were three men in my early life who taught me how to play it. The first one was my Boy Scout leader, a man who served as a navigator in the First World War. He started a fife and drum corps and I joined. There were about eight or ten of us and we used to march in parades.

My next music teacher was Larry Pettingill. He was a graduate of the Boston Conservatory of Music and had returned to Mattawamkeag to live with his parents because of his health though I never learned just why. He could play the accordion and nearly anything with strings or keys. He liked to teach kids how to play instruments, and since harmonicas were relatively inexpensive he bought every one of us a harmonica and taught us how to play them. Well, in no time at all he built up a harmonica band, with nearly 20 kids of all ages. We were good; at least I think we were. We were even asked to play on the radio in Bangor. Most of us had never seen a city except perhaps in the movies. Over the next couple of years we must have played over the radio station at least twice a year. It was a great thrill.

Around the same time I was learning to play the harmonica an elderly man, who had been a marching band player in his early days, gave me his trumpet. It had seen much former use, but it still could be played. He also gave me a well-worn book, *Teach Yourself To Play The Trumpet*, which I took to like a dog goes for a fresh bone. I read that book until the pages near fell apart and taught myself how to read music. The only other music I had beyond the book was a hymnal so I learned to play all the hymns too. I played night and day even though the neighbors very nicely asked if I could play only in the daytime.

Nearly every small town throughout the whole country, including our town, had a grange, a social organization for farm folk. The grange held dances and brought in bands from the cities. I got the idea that if I could find enough locals who played some instrument, we could become a dance band and it wouldn't cost the grange nearly as much money.

I kept up with the trumpet. One friend got a hold of a saxophone, another friend came up with a trombone, and we started trying to play some of the popular music of the time, big band dance music. There was a middle-aged guy who was a fantastic piano player. He taught himself, which was so common back in small rural towns. Larry Pettingill was open to helping us start a dance band. It wasn't long before the towns-people began to know of us, and we were soon engaged to play for the Mattawamkeag Grange Dances every Saturday night during the summer.

Some folk might say we weren't much of a band, but we were happy to be able to provide sufficient music for people in the town to have a good time. We called ourselves the *Agitators*. I thought up the name because I always thought of dancing as stirring people up, and that's what we did.

There were five of us regulars. I played the trumpet, as well as a well-used snare drum, a bass drum, and a set of cymbals. I wasn't the best drum player, but at least I could keep time. George Anthony "Chewy Junior" played the saxophone. Bill Adams played the trombone. Mickey McCafferty was a lively pianist, playing entirely by ear. Our best player, of course, was Larry Pettingill, playing nearly everything: violin, guitar, accordion, banjo, harmonica, and just about anything else. I never quite understood why he hadn't gone further with his music, but we never questioned his motives. He was a fine person and an excellent musician and that was all that mattered to us.

As a dance band we received $5 each for four hours of playing. That may not seem like very much, but I had just returned from a 55-hour week with the railroad getting only $12 for the whole week's work. Five dollars seemed like a gold strike.

We played from eight until midnight and sometimes longer. We always played a mix of fox trots, waltzes and contra dances. My sisters taught me how to waltz so I loved waltzes. A contra dance was our name for a reel. Everybody in the hall got into those and when they were finished all of us had to take a good break.

Occasionally a few dancers took a trip outside to cool down or have a sip of alcohol. The town constable was always standing at the door to keep everyone in order, and those who did not seem of proper nature were asked kindly not to enter.

Back in those days boys usually sat on one side of the hall and girls sat on the other. It seemed to me that both groups were kind of bashful about getting up to dance. But when a contra dance started, if you were sitting there usually some rather large woman would come by and grab you, but it was fun. Sometimes the piano player would play the contra dance solo so I could get out and do some dancing, which I loved to do.

War Arrives by Train

We lived through the Great Depression, yet it was as if it had not touched our town. We weren't fancy, but we were warm in the winter and had plenty to eat. When World War II started in Europe, again we didn't notice a difference, because nothing much seemed to change in our little corner of the world. When we went to the Saturday matinee we'd see the newsreels showing the war in Europe and a lot about a man named Hitler who seemed to want to take over all of Europe. He had already led his Nazi troops in taking over Poland, France, Belgium, and the Netherlands, and now he was bombing England. We seemed to be quite far removed from all of that.

Then we noticed the number of freight trains coming through our little town doubled; there was more freight being hauled to Halifax, and then shipped on to England. Our town was the junction of two railroad lines, the Maine Central Railroad connecting central Maine to Boston, and the Canadian Pacific Railroad, connecting Maine to all of Canada all the way to the Pacific. It was also a direct connection to all of Europe via the city of Halifax, Nova Scotia. That was our contact with the rest of America and the rest of the world really.

Then the U.S. Army sent a company of black soldiers to our town to prevent sabotage of the two railroad bridges that brought the two railroads through our town. We hardly knew what sabotaging meant or why anyone would want to do such a thing, but every

English children evacuees headed for Canadian farms, Mattawamkeag railroad station, Maine 1939

night when we sat down to listen to the six o'clock news we would hear more about what the Germans were doing and it didn't sound very good.

Some people might think that black soldiers might cause a northern Maine town a bit of consternation, but the people of the town opened their homes to them, invited them in to Sunday dinners. We used to make popcorn balls and divinity fudge for them and everyone had a real good time. A favorite entertainment in those days was just sitting around a piano and singing. Not every home had such an instrument, but those who did often invited the soldiers into their homes and you never heard such beautiful singing as came out of those times.

The war continued and the trains kept coming. When the 8 o'clock passenger train came through every night from Halifax often people from Europe would be on board. The train stopped in our town while the engine was filling up with water and coal. Passengers came into the station where there was a nice hot stove. We heard different languages; it was fascinating for us kids. Half the kids in town would go to the train station just to see the train come in and the people on it.

One night in 1939 Marm and Dad were with us waiting for the train to come in, which was a bit unusual for them. When the train stopped a bunch of windows suddenly popped opened from three of the train cars and kids started sticking their heads out of the windows. Marm asked the conductor who they were and he told us they were kids from England who were being sent to farms in Canada to save them from being killed by the German bombs that were dropping all over England.

We had never seen so many kids. They could all speak English but their English was a bit different from ours. Well, it didn't take long before we were in real conversation with those kids. They were not allowed to get off the train. I can still see them all hanging so far out of those windows. We all had questions about each other, and you can imagine just how much talking there was going on in that short 30 minutes while the engine was filling up with water and coal.

It didn't take long before we found out there would be more of them coming along. So Marm got an idea (she was always full of ideas) that the kids in our church youth group and their families should make goodies for the next load of English kids. The very next night, sure enough there was another train with English kids on it. Instead of just talking with those kids, we began handing out popcorn balls, fudge, and even sandwiches, lemonade and Kool-Aid drinks. Many of those trains stopped in our town. In the fall the temperature was beginning to drop down quite rapidly, so Marm thought up the idea to give the kids mittens and scarves. Every night for about a year we met the eight o'clock train. Sometimes we'd go and there wouldn't be any refugee kids on the train and we'd be very disappointed. That was our touch with the war until Dad got a new job.

Down to the Sea

The war kept getting worse. The United States hadn't entered the war yet, but they were making planes and bombs and shipping them to England and Russia. We heard they were going to build ships in South Portland and they needed lots of men and even women to work. Dad, as well as being an expert woodsman, was also a pretty good carpenter, and carpenters were badly needed in shipbuilding. Even though the ships were mostly made of metal, carpenters would build all of the framework and construction forms before the welders put the metals together. So there went my dad, far away from home.

About a month or so after he moved to Portland, Dad decided it would be wise for all of us to make the move to Portland. By then it was just Marm, my sister Ada, and me at home since all my older brothers and sisters had started off on their own by then. Moving to a big city and big school sure made me nervous. I had just finished my junior year at Mattawamkeag High School in a class of only eight kids. My new school in Portland, I heard by the grapevine, had over 300 kids in the senior class alone.

Soon Dad sent us a letter saying he found an apartment in the city of Portland right on a bus line, so he could easily get to and from the shipyard in South Portland. Marm found a man with a truck who would move us, though we didn't own very much furniture. All this activity was exciting to me, to leave a town of less than 1,000 people, where we had all we needed to be happy and move to a city we'd never even visited with around 60,000 people.

Since Dad was already working at the shipyard, Marm arranged for our move. I worked two summers on the extra gang with the railroad laying steel between Greenville and Jackman and had just come home from my last week there. The hired truck arrived to take our meager belongings and us to our new place by the sea. I was excited, but somewhat apprehensive. Dad found us a flat or apartment above a laundry right on busy Congress Street. We had everything we needed — each other.

Dad, with Marm, before heading off to work at the South Portland Shipyard, Portland, 1942

I didn't have much time to get settled after our move; school began in a week. Portland High school was nearly a mile from our flat. We were surprised to see the school was not just a big square building as I had imagined, but a monstrosity three stories high with three massive wings.

Inside we found a sign that read, *Office*. A very business-like lady approached us and asked if she could help. I told her I wanted to enroll in school and a rather interesting look came over her face. She asked me where I came from. When I told her she heaved a rather big sigh and said, "You must be one of those shipyard worker's kid. Is that right?" The way she said it made me feel I had done something wrong.

I answered up weakly, "Yes, I am," even though inside I felt just a little bit proud of being a shipyard worker's son.

Marm spoke right up in her motherly but firm voice, "Yes, we are and I want my son to get enrolled here in the senior class."

Well, that caused the lady to take another look at Marm. In a rather subdued voice she began asking questions. "Did you bring his records?" Of course we had forgotten we might need my records, but Marm told her we had not had time for that but she would soon have them sent. I wasn't even sure Mattawamkeag High School had my records.

Later on I found out why the lady in the office had been somewhat snotty when she suggested I might be "one of those shipyard worker's kids." Many families like ours had come to work in the shipyard. Portland was nearly overrun with so many new families and sometimes we were put down.

I remember seeing my father in his work coveralls waiting for the bus to take him to the shipyard in South Portland. Very few people owned cars so the buses were always loaded and quite often many people had to ride standing up. One morning my dad was one of the first to get on the bus before it started to fill. There were no seats left when an elderly lady got on the bus and started looking for a seat.

He stood up and said, "Would you like to have this?"

She looked at him and said, "I'm not going to sit there. That's dirty. You shipyard workers get everything dirty."

My father was one of the nicest men you ever saw, and I was proud of the work he did. Perhaps the schools and the people of Portland were not quite ready for the influx of new folks.

Although I lived in Maine, a coastal state, for nearly 16 years I still had not seen the Atlantic Ocean. My love for geography had taken me pretty much all around the world, in my imagination way. I was with Columbus on his voyages, and Magellan when he discovered the Marianas Island. I was with Sir Francis Drake going around the globe. I had a fascination with the oceans and with sailing. It was my love of poetry that first took me to the sea with John Masefield. On Fridays in school we all had to recite a poem, and that's how *Sea Fever* became one of my favorites: "I must go down to the seas again, to the lonely sea and the sky…" Now, here I was, living in the big city of Portland right on the Atlantic Ocean.

As a *hick* from northern Maine I found the city fascinating and spent much time exploring its many side streets and learning its history. Portland is the birthplace of one of my favorite poets, Henry Wadsworth Longfellow. It is also a seaport with a beautiful and bountiful harbor. Its history goes way back to the times of explorers like Champlain, Captain John Smith, Fernando Gorges and many others. Portland was formerly named Falmouth, and long ago was nearly destroyed by the British who set it on fire.

On my walks from school on Congress Street and Cumberland Avenue I often took the long way home. At first Marm was a bit concerned about my absences, but I think she was accustomed to my wanderings and exploring in the woods during my younger days. Of course a city is quite different from the forest. In the forest the only thing to worry about are bears, and bears mostly avoid people. But in a city there are other things that cause consternation; surely one had to be a bit more on guard.

This may sound odd but I was concerned about buses. I had never seen so many buses, and they all seemed to be rushing and stopping. You had to be on watch all the time for people rushing to catch a bus or a bus pulling out right in heavy traffic. Congress Street in particular was extremely busy with all kinds of traffic. As a kid from a small town where it was unusual to see more than two or three cars or trucks at a time, you can understand my country-boy concern. There was so much activity going on in Portland and every day there seemed to be more and more. I never took a bus, for one thing I hardly ever had any money, and secondly, I have to admit, I was just a little bit fearful of them.

My wanderings took me to a park called Deering Oaks. It certainly was well named since there were many remarkable huge oak trees that must have been there since the Revolutionary War. In the center, was a lovely pond with a duck house and lots of ducks. You could rent a small rowboat and paddle all around. There were benches and places to walk everywhere. The next thing that caught my eye was a tennis court. I loved to play tennis but Mattawamkeag had only one tennis court that belonged to the boss at the mill and no one could play on that. Although, I have to admit when the boss's family was on vacation a few of us would sneak on and play to our hearts' content. Tennis became one of my most loved games and much of it really began right there at Deering Oaks.

My next wanderings took me to the Western and Eastern Promenades. I knew the word *promenade* meant to walk but I was amazed at how extensive and beautiful they were and how much you could see from the heights overlooking the bay. Our home was near the Western

Promenade, high up on a ridge overlooking the harbor and towards the mountains westward. It became a place of dreaming for me.

Journeying up Munjoy Hill, where Congress Street comes to an end, I came to the Eastern Promenade and the Atlantic Ocean. It was my first glimpse of that stretch of water that, unbeknownst to me at that time, in just another year I would be sailing over.

The top of Munjoy Hill was filled with lovely houses originally settled by sea captains and their families. Since the captains were often away from home for months at a time without any reliable means of communication, they built a cupola on top of the house, usually encased with windows, so that any time of the year the wife could be on watch for her husband's ship to enter the bay. These structures were called a *widows walk* indicating that the captain might not even return home because of the tremendous dangers at sea. How lonely those times must have been with no means of communication between loved ones. Truly there was a great amount of sadness and difficulty in those earlier days. (Little did I know, soon many wives and mothers and sisters would be wondering when their men would return home from the seas, home from the war.)

As I continued my exploration around the Eastern Promenade there was another eye-catcher, a beautiful park again, overlooked by old and gnarled, but sturdy oaks, maples, and elm trees. The trees looked as if they were standing guard over the scene before my eyes. Ships! Ships of many kinds. As I walked slowly around the Promenade, taking in every feature of it on the ground, as well as out over the bay, I soon came to the memorial of the Maine, a battleship that made history in the Spanish American War. As I circled through the park still gazing across the water, my eyes could not miss, far across the harbor, the shipyard where Dad was working. It appeared to be an immense operation.

Back in my West End neighborhood I met people who were different from me. On my way to school I often walked down Congress Street with black students, several who played in the marching band with me. I also met Italian kids who lived in tenement buildings in the Back Bay area. I met Armenian, Jewish, Greek and even a few French kids. As a boy from the North Country I was not accustomed to those different cultures. My observations are only those of a Maine boy whose life was rapidly being exposed to a different sort of life.

Gee, I Wish I Were a Man, I'd Join the Navy

Portland was caught up in a war atmosphere. All one had to do was to walk down Congress Street in the evenings to see the place was afloat with sailors. Standing on the top of Munjoy Hill looking down at the city, it looked like white waves because there were so many sailors walking in the streets with their white caps on. It was an exciting time.

Casco Bay was filled with so many ships some said you could walk from one ship to another and cross the bay. Portland provided one of the best ports along the upper part of the Atlantic coast. The peninsula of Portland curved around and protruded out into the ocean, yet it was protected by several islands in Casco Bay. The bay provided excellent protection for ocean-going vessels.

Portland has long carried a history of shipping. It was a major shipping port during West Indian trade and even to China during the 1800s. In 1941, Portland once again took on another kind of trade. By then, the war in Europe was already deep in action. England had suffered some phases of defeat. Russia had turned away from Germany and was under attack. Norway and other Baltic Sea countries were already under German power. The United States was surely aware of how close we might be to being considered Hitler's next victim. German U-boats had been sighted off our coasts. We were eagerly attempting to help our allies by shipping war materials and food supplies.

Cargo ships headed up the coast laden with supplies but with no defense. As soon as they left the protection of their supply ports, they were open to the attacks of enemy warships. The best protection for them was to travel together in convoys preferably with a warship or the coast guard alongside to protect them. Portland was the final base for warships, battleships, destroyers, and cruisers before joining a convoy.

Anyone who was caught up in that era of change knew their own lives would never be the same. I saw myself growing into manhood, finishing high school, hopefully going on to some sort of higher education, finding employment, getting married, having children and a home. Such was the life I had grown up with, a happy safe atmosphere.

December 7, 1941 changed everyone's life in our country. Who would have believed that a little country like Japan would be so foolish as to attack us, a big strong opponent? Even though the attack was way off in Hawaii it struck home. Some of our Maine boys were on those ships and the airfield that the Japanese had bombed. We now had to declare war against Japan, that little country that we had been sending scrap iron to for years; little knowing they were using it to build implements of war. Certainly the shock was felt all over our country. To those of us in Portland, who were already part of the war in Europe through our shipbuilding and cargo ships, we now were a part of a war on both sides of our country.

Within just a few months, our heretofore rather quiet lives took on dramatic changes. Our government rapidly took measures to step up preparations to defend our country as well as the countries of the world that were being taken over by military powers on both sides of the globe. Certainly, we were now in a world war. Japan had already taken over much of China and the Malaysian countries and now was attacking the Philippine Islands. They had complete control of most of the islands in the Pacific Ocean and would undoubtedly attack our Hawaiian Islands again. They were already approaching Alaska. We weren't ready.

Deering Oaks Park, particularly in the wintertime, was one of the favorite places for young teenagers in Portland because it had a beautiful skating pond. Quite often that's where you might meet a gal, but the girls were all looking for sailors and guys in uniform. I think maybe that was why I wanted to go into the Navy.

Two of my brothers had left college and enlisted in the Air Force. My oldest brother was already stationed in England. My sister left college and enlisted in the Navy. When I turned 16 I wanted to enlist, but I had to have parental permission. I graduated in 1942 and I really wanted to join the military, but my parents still wouldn't let me sign up.

I heard they were hiring over at the shipyard and paying good money, what we considered good money in those days anyway. I went over and they asked me how old I was. I said I was 18 and filled out the papers. They gave me a job and put me on the graveyard shift from 11 at night to seven in the morning. We were building three or four Liberty Ships at one time. It was an exciting place and the pay was good. I worked there for two weeks. Then I was called into the office one night.

My boss said, "I'm sorry, you can't work here anymore."

I asked, "Why not?"

"You lied about your age. You have to be 18." He had filed my social security number and must have found that I was 17, so he fired me.

After that I got a job in a hardware store, but my mother insisted I go to college. We had no money. I didn't know much about loans in those days. I had saved $250. She said, "Go and see if they will take you."

It was August. I hitchhiked all the way to the University of Maine in Orono. I went to the enrollment office, and was told they would take me in. I told them I only had $250. They still accepted me.

I wasn't enthusiastic at all about college. I had no car. I tried to go home to Portland every weekend by hitchhiking. When I turned 18 in November I didn't have to get parental permission anymore, so I said to myself, "I'm going to join the Navy."

I went to the Navy recruiting office. They took one look at me and said, "How is your eyesight?"

I said, "Well, 20/40."

"I'm sorry, you've got to have at least 20/30."

So I went to the Air Force and they looked at me and said, "What's your eyesight?" You can guess where that got me.

It's interesting. There's a certain amount of attraction to the uniform. The Navy and the Marines, of course, had fancy uniforms, but the Army didn't have good-looking uniforms, and I never bothered to enlist with the Army, figuring they wouldn't take me anyway. Since I couldn't enlist I thought well, I must keep on with college. I started my second semester. Then I got a letter from President Roosevelt calling me up to go into service.

I still had to go and take a physical. Physically, I was in top shape. I just couldn't see very well. They put me in the infantry. We used to say, "You don't need to see in the Army. You just need to be strong enough to carry a 60 pound pack, a 10 pound rifle, 2 pounds of ammo and do a 20 mile forced march in just 2 hours."

That's how I got in the Army.

PART II: MAINE BOY GOES TO WAR

You'll Know When You Get There

When I left home for my induction into the army I suspected I would not be able to come back home, so I said my goodbyes to Marm and Dad, and headed to the city hall in Portland at four o'clock in the afternoon. There were 50 or more of us there, and a sergeant pushing people around. They passed around little bottles and somebody said, "What's that for?"

The sergeant said, "You piss in it."

They gave us a urine test and a rough physical and then they swore us in. We stood up and took the oath that we would give our lives for our country, a promise I always remembered each time I entered combat.

They marched us the whole length of Congress Street to Union Station never telling us where we were going. I didn't know it yet, but if you ask an officer, "Where are we going?" the answer is always, "You'll know when you get there."

At Union Station, around 5 o'clock at night they boarded us on a train, 50 of us jammed into one passenger car, and we headed off into the night toward somewhere. The train stopped a few times before we finally arrived at our destination. None of us knew what was going on. I figured we were probably going to a military base.

We arrived at Fort Devens in Massachusetts around nine o'clock at night. It was snowing and wet and cold, and all we had on were our *civvies* (civilian clothes). They took us into this massive building with hundreds and hundreds more guys and a bunch of officers.

I noticed piles of civilian clothing. We were told to strip, put our names and addresses on the tags on our clothes and put them in the pile. It was March and it was cold; we were shivering and naked.

There were lines of guys stripped standing before some officers and a doctor. We stood in these long lines for a very long, long time. The doctor was examining each man. The next thing I knew somebody was jabbing me with needles. I got four or five different shots in my arm. I didn't know what was happening because I couldn't see what was going on in front of the line. I came before another officer he said, "Turn around and spread your cheeks." I guess they were looking for disease.

We didn't get our uniforms until we passed the tests. They led us off into another section where there were these two corporals who issued our uniforms. They measured our feet. In the infantry feet are the most important part of the body. Then, they started throwing clothing at us: two pairs of pants, two shirts, an overcoat, and a duffel bag. We dressed quickly and they marched us out in the cold and into the barracks. By then it was about midnight.

In the barracks there was a buck sergeant telling us, "Get these blankets and that pillow. I'll show you how to make an army bed." One thing about the military, when they give somebody a little bit of authority they take all of it. I mean, possibly they've never had this opportunity, so they scream at you and shout. The buck sergeant showed us how to make a military bed. We made it, and if he didn't like it, he'd strip it and we'd make it again and so forth. We finally got to go to bed around one o'clock. I immediately fell asleep.

The next morning I awoke around five to roaring and yelling and screaming. "Get up and get out there." Somebody asked why. "You'll know it when you get out there."

They told us to line up, though we'd had no practice at how to line up. "If your name is called step out." We found out this was "*shipping call*." Some guys had been there for two or three days already and were getting assigned to camps. We'd have to wait three days for our assignments. In the meantime, we did KP, that's Kitchen Police or Kitchen Patrol, which meant cleaning pots and peeling potatoes.

On the third day, it was cold, snowy, and hardly even daylight at five a.m. when they called my name. "Go and get your duffel bags and meet right here in ten minutes." Next thing we knew we were being marched off to a rail depot and put on trains. Duffle bags over shoulders, somewhere near a 100 of us boys, now about to be changed into men, headed for the train depot for our first long distance train ride to *somewhere*.

The train took off and again we didn't know our destination. When we asked, we always got the same answer, and not in a nice way.

Apparently the non-commissioned officers felt they had to bark and growl to get command. On the converted passenger cars they squeezed three men and their duffle bags into seats that normally accommodated two people.

We could tell by the sun that we were headed west. Rumors are a great part of being in the Army.

"Where are we going?"

"Well, we're going west."

"Does that mean we're going to be shipped out to the Pacific?"

The Pacific area was directly ahead of us, even though it was still 5,000 miles away; it seemed the most logical place for us to go. Then another rumor arose that seemed even worse: Alaska. Rumor had it the Japs had landed in Alaska. We figured we were probably stopping off somewhere in the Rockies to get accustomed to cold weather and lots of ice and snow before heading to the Great White North.

Normally a bunch of young men always have much to talk about, so much that they all want to talk at once. But there seemed to be very little to talk about other than rumors. We knew we were going to be trained to fight in the infantry. We didn't know where or when and we weren't very excited about it. I mostly spent the next five days writing to Marm and taking photos of the scenes out the window with my little box camera.

We went through towns in New York and Ohio. When our train stopped in St. Louis we were allowed to get off and walk around. The American Red Cross met us with coffee and doughnuts. We had a layover in St. Louis for a day. They shoved our train cars off into the stockyards out of the way. The stockyard atmosphere was not the best, but neither was the train car. There were cattle staying in the stockyards with us, what seemed like thousands of them, bellowing all night.

It seemed that every time we stopped someone somehow brought on board sufficient bags of food for all of us. All we had to do was line up and walk to the end of the car and get our bag of food rations for the day, which held all three meals within it. Of course none of it was hot or recently-prepared food, but in the infantry we had to get used to cold bagged-up meals because often that's all we'd get for several weeks, and sometimes more.

There were toilets on the car, but with 50 guys in there it was impossible. So the train had to pull off every now and then so that we could relieve ourselves.

The next stop was St. Paul, Minnesota, so we knew we were going west. It was nighttime when we got going again and the rumors going around were that we were headed west. When the sun came up, I noticed the sun was rising just a bit to my left.

I said, "The sun is coming up in the east! That means we are going south."

The rumors started up again.

"That's not the direction of Colorado or Idaho or North Dakota."

"That means we're not going to Alaska or the Pacific."

"But where else?"

There was more chatter than we had heard for quite awhile.

Then someone said, "We are going into hot country. I'll bet they're going to send us to Africa. I heard the campaign has started there. We've got to train in hot country to get ready for that."

About four o'clock in the afternoon, our train began to slow down. I looked out the windows and saw soldiers marching by, a couple of jeeps and a station house. The train stopped. A sergeant came into our car and announced, "You are at Camp Joseph T. Robinson in Arkansas, the Basic Infantry Replacement Training Center. You will be assigned to your sleeping quarters where you will wait for further orders."

Oh, Happy Day! We had arrived!

Camp Robinson

We arrived at Camp Robinson early in the morning, at the crack of dawn. Our guide, a snappy sergeant, directed us to our accommodations. I expected barracks, but was pleasantly surprised to find many small hut-like structures that accommodated six men each. These huts were our homes for eight weeks. Seeing that little hut immediately brought me back to Mattawamkeag to our tarpaper shack. That little hut looked pretty good to me. We were ordered to put our duffle bags at the foot of one of the bunks and await further orders.

Whenever we were told what to do by one of our superiors, those words were not just a bit of information; they were *orders*. A good soldier soon learned when an order was given it required immediate results, no questions asked. For example, say someone gave you an order and you answered, "But I thought…"

The immediately reply, "You're not here to think. I will do the thinking for you. You are here only to obey, and obey immediately."

It always amazed me how fast a new recruit learned that lesson.

Growing up in a family such as mine with seven children living in very close quarters we had un-written rules to live by. However, our rules were not imposed roughly on us. Instead, our parents set the example of what rules to follow, and love was always the best rule to live by. In the Army, I had to learn a new way of following rules. The first few days of training were geared toward teaching us how to follow orders from superiors. Free living had come to an end. There were a lot of rules to learn.

My new life as a *fresh* private (that's a new recruit) was filled from dawn to dusk with rules, routine, and orders. No more waking up to Marm's sweet voice, "Paul it's time to get up, I have a delicious breakfast waiting for you." At the break of dawn, I heard what sounded like a 100 horns all playing a questionable piece of music. I later found out that only one bugle played Reveille over loudspeakers placed all over the army base; the echoes all clashing with one another. At that sound everyone clambered to immediately get up, get dressed, wash and shave.

Paul Marshall practicing rifle training,
Camp Robinson, 1943

We shaved every day, whether or not we had any growth of a beard.

"Fall in!" That was the first order, meaning to take your place, always the same one, in the line up. "Attention." In just a matter of seconds we had to form a line. (Of course there are always a few men who could never seem to take their place immediately. They were put on the *shit list*, which usually meant they would be doing KP that day.) The corporal or sergeant in charge passed along the lines of men. He stood barely a foot from my face. He might even rub his hand on someone's chin and speak in a snarling voice, "You did not shave this morning. Ten demerits." This daily routine is called *Inspection*. Every morning our shoes had to be shined to a mirror-like perfection, our buttons all buttoned, our eyes straight ahead, our caps on straight, our brass belt buckles shining.

The next bugle call was known as *mess call*. I found that to be an interesting title because I knew a *mess* as a state of complete confusion. I soon came to learn however that the mess hall was perhaps the cleanest building in camp, thanks to those of us on KP duty. "No talking at meals! You are here only to eat," a superior would yell at us, meaning get it over with and get ready for the next order.

Next up was barracks inspections. That meant my bed should be made tight enough that the inspection officer could flip a coin on it. My second pair of boots (I was wearing my first pair) had to be placed in an exact place just under the foot of my bed. Both pairs had better

Parade ground, Camp Robinson, 1943

put forth a shine that would make the inspection officer blink his eyes. My footlocker, in which I kept my personal things as well as one complete uniform change, had better be open to display everything *in the right place*. There had better not be a speck of dirt *anywhere* in the barracks. It always surprised me that the inspecting officer could find a small speck of dust, big enough to give you ten demerits.

During morning inspection everyone got placed on some kind of detail, which could be anything from KP to latrine duty, to parade ground duty, (i.e. picking up cigarette butts). During your duties, privates might be charged ten demerits for no particular reason. If I uttered even a sigh I would immediately be given five more demerits. The parade field, of course, was always littered with cigarette butts, since everyone smokes during their breaks. After each break everyone throws his butt on the ground. You can imagine what the field looked like at the end of a day. But picking up cigarette butts was another way to work off demerits.

Every morning we endured physical training exercises to prepare us to withstand weeks of extreme physical strain during combat. The exercises we did in high school and college were nothing compared to the calisthenics of basic training. At least once a day we marched wearing full field packs in parade formation. We had to obey special commands and learn intricate maneuvers designed to move troops from one place to another. I learned to *quickstep*, which is running in a smooth movement. Some days we marched ten miles carrying a full field pack and rifle without stopping for rest.

I was issued a rifle and was instructed to treat it as if it was my beloved companion. I had to strip it down, piece by piece, then put it back together again, and do it fast and efficiently. Whenever we heard the order *present arms* we had to present our rifles for inspection. It had to be perfect, no dust, no extra oil; both metal and wood parts had to shine. (In real combat I chuckled to remember this emphasis on perfectly shined rifles for the mud of battle stripped any polish I could apply.)

Every day we spent time on the range shooting at targets with our rifles and stabbing at things with our bayonets. We crawled across a field on our hands and knees while machine guns fired overhead. Gravel mounds exploded around us as we crawled, plastering us with dirt. I didn't even know if the guns fired live shells or blanks, but I was too afraid to rise up to find out. When I reached the battlefields of Europe I was glad I had had this experience because I was accustomed to the bouncing artillery shells. This training probably saved my life.

There was no such thing as spare time in basic training. There was a building called the day room. Though there was very little time during the day to take advantage of that room; if I did not have detail to attend to in the evening I could spend a bit of time there. The only pieces of furniture in the room were a couple of ping pong tables. If you had never played ping pong you simply had to learn how in basic training, as that was the only game available in the day room. I became an expert at ping pong. The two most popular games played during free time, other than ping pong, were poker and shooting craps (rolling dice). Poker and craps were gambling games played for money. Stakes were not very high, considering that the monthly pay of a private was just $21 a month.

I also became a perpetual smoker in basic. Just about everyone eventually became a smoker. You almost had to smoke or be looked upon as some sort of a "different kind of a person." In combat, when several days rations were passed out there was always a small bag of cigarette packages included in each supply of rations, whether one smoked or not.

There was a store on the base called the Post Exchange, where soldiers with a bit of time off could drop in and have a Coke or even a beer, or buy cigarettes or candy bars or toilet articles. On a private's pay of $21 dollars each month there were very few things I could afford to buy.

When we were not in training, we slept, some times even six or seven hours at night at most. Sometimes there might be as much as an hour before *Taps* was played on the echoing loudspeakers, signaling the end of the day. I found those rare free moments in the evening a good time to write letters home. I had to write in the dark with a very small flashlight so the sergeant couldn't see it. I did not want my parents to worry about me and tried to have them believe that I enjoyed being in the army. I began each letter with the sentence: "Don't worry about me, I'm okay."

Basic training rapidly changed us from boys to men. You often had to subdue your feelings and complaints or be accused of griping, which would not put you in good standing with your superiors. Even though I was surrounded by hundreds of other soldiers I was often lonely. I learned that one could be lonely, even in a crowd. It was easy to reminisce the happy times of my childhood. I don't think I was alone in these feelings, but we didn't share our feelings easily with others. I remember there was a lack of openness with each other. It is hard to put this into words, but we were all very much aware that we came from different backgrounds. It kept us from sharing our common lives. A few of us were from New England, though very few from the kind of rural background I came from. Many were from the New York City area. There were Jewish boys and Italian boys and Irish boys, and Greek boys and even Armenian boys. We were all Americans of course. But everyone pretty much kept to people who shared a common lingo. A few of the men were older than most of us, maybe by about ten years or so. Most of us recent draftees had just turned 18. Those who were 28 or 30 years old seemed so much older than us.

We made some friends, but kept our distance too. You never knew who might end up on the casualty list. Yet, there was also a sense of brotherhood that was essential. We knew we were all replacements, merely hole-fillers sent where we were needed most.

Another condition that seemed to prevent close relationships was the fact that there was hardly any time. From Reveille until Taps our life was rush, rush, rush! Rush here! Line up there! And no talking! Occasionally on a long march we had a few minutes to converse, but the ten-minute breaks gave us only enough time to light up our cigarettes, have a drink from our canteens, and scout out a spot for a quick latrine break.

There were few opportunities to get out of camp and enjoy life. I sent $10 of my salary home each month to help my parents, which left me with only $11. At the time it seemed to be enough. In the eight weeks of basic I had three weekend passes, which I spent in Little Rock, the capital of Arkansas. It seemed to be a pretty nice city but I was still a country boy and somewhat wary of cities. They told us to watch out for pickpockets and loose women.

During basic training they showed us many movies for training purposes, mostly about combat, but some of the films were quite different. Almost once a week and some times more, we were subjected to films about venereal disease, a term I had never even heard of before. Those films did not just *talk* about a disease; they *showed* very clearly how a disease could be contracted and what it could do to your body. They depicted the kind of women we should be on the look out for. I didn't like to watch those films and always felt somewhat embarrassed doing so.

When we were on *pass*, it was like being in a different world than camp. There were lots of bars and places of entertainment. I did not care to frequent them, partly because I did not have the money, but also those places were not of "our world." I had known a pretty different life in Maine. My family didn't drink alcohol, and my interactions with females had been confined to school and the neighborhood. All of a sudden I had to confront this new environment. I had to make choices with these new freedoms. I sometimes felt I was simply on a tour in some strange place I didn't really want to be.

Aside from the bars and such there were other, very often more rewarding, places for servicemen to meet people to help them with their loneliness. At the USO (United Service Organization), you could find *hostesses*, young women happy to dance or play games, or simply listen and talk with a lonely serviceman. A supervising elder person screened these young women. They were escorted from their homes by taxi, and when the evening was over at a decent hour they were escorted back home in the same manner. If a girl was interested in one of the servicemen, it was appropriate to invite him home for dinner with her family. Three of my sisters were hostesses in Portland and a few of their guests fit right into our family. One of them eventually became my brother-in-law.

At the USO servicemen could come and even spend the night if needed. There was always a hot cup of coffee, soft drinks, and often sandwiches and sweets. It was a place to write letters or listen to music or merely rest. You could send home telegrams or make telephone calls, read, or talk with a hostess. Often there was dancing in the evenings. These USO stations were usually set up at railroad stations making it very handy for the traveling servicemen. Many of them provided cots and blankets for spending the night or a nap while waiting for a train. If there were performances going on in the city usually you could get a free ticket to the show.

The reason I have been so strong on explaining this wonderful opportunity for the lonely serviceman is that the person chosen to be the director of the Portland USO was my mother! After watching four of her children leave home for war she felt very strongly that this would be her contribution to their efforts. Whenever she saw a lonely serviceman, she immediately saw one of her own children in him. Her experience during those difficult times helped her get through the temporary loss of her own children.

Three times during my training before going overseas I took the opportunity to come home for a short visit, never telling Mother

I was coming, hoping to surprise her when I walked into the USO at Union Station.

She became a temporary mother to hundreds of servicemen. They would send her letters, Christmas cards, and Easter cards expressing their gratitude to her for "being there" when they needed someone to love them. Even after the war servicemen would come from their homes in far off states just to visit my mother who was their *mother in absentia*.

As I look back over those eight weeks I wonder why no one explained the goals and purpose of basic training, and how it was conducted. Why were we subjected to such de-personalizing procedures? I have concluded the *destruction of personality*, as I have termed it, was to make us into a unit, a team working together toward our goal. We were not a group of individuals anymore. There was no room for individuality, only obedience to commands from a superior who had been trained and chosen to lead. The parts of an army could not operate entirely on their own, only as a unit all directed toward the same goal.

I still have the small booklet they gave us during induction. The first contents of this little book included the order of rank. As privates we were the lowest on the ladder. The next rank up was private first class. You could easily remain a private for the entire war, but usually after eight weeks of basic training you were raised to the rank of private first class. Very little power came with that rank. The only reward was an extra $10 a month, raising our monthly income to $30.

Higher ranks in order were: corporal, "buck" sergeant, staff sergeant, tech sergeant, first sergeant, and finally the top rank, master sergeant. All those ranks were under the heading of non-commissioned officers. The next levels of command were termed the commissioned officers: second lieutenant, first lieutenant, captain, major, lieutenant colonel, colonel, and then the four grades of general. We had to salute whenever coming in contact with anyone from this group. It didn't take long to recognize the insignia of each rank and learn to obey their orders.

Every soldier must accept that it is his unit, not his individual talents, that will be most effective in combat. Still, the treatment issued by our superiors was difficult to take. At inspection time if you did not shape up your hut-mates also paid the price. If during parade time you did not keep in step your whole unit looked bad. Even on KP duty it was necessary to do your part. The Army had a term for a soldier who didn't do his part, a *goldbrick*, which literally meant a brick that looks like gold but is actually worthless. There never seemed to be much written about the methods and the intent of basic training. The new soldier just learned the hard way.

I did learn the value of having pride in your unit. I was an important part of a unit and just as responsible for it as any other member. I am still proud that I was a member of the 104th Infantry Division, even though I never made a rank higher than private first class. I am still proud that I was a part of a country that helped save the world, even though my part in it was a mere a drop in the bucket.

College Life

Our eight weeks in basic training seemed to drag at first, but we became so busy time moved along rather rapidly. Soon we were wondering what would come next. Most of us assumed we'd be assigned to some infantry division headed for combat. Those who had volunteered might get a choice, but most of us draftees had no choice as to where we might go.

One week before the end of basic training we were given a written exam, similar to an IQ test. If you scored 120 or more, you were sent into a new program called the ASTP (Army Specialized Training Program). I passed the test.

For those of us fortunate enough to achieve the desired IQ level this opportunity came as a gift from heaven. This meant we had choices. We could become commissioned officers. We would not have to serve in the infantry, and possibly, not even have to face combat situations. We would still be able to complete our college studies.

The rest of the unit was granted a week's furlough to go home, but the ASTP candidates were scheduled to ship out right away.

"Where next?"

"Just wait. You will know when you get there. Be ready at 8 a.m. tomorrow."

We were ready! "Fall in. Forward march." Duffel bags and all.

At the closing ceremony, all units came out in full dress and marched all around the parade field, like a high school graduation. The camp band led the way and all units marched before the officer's stand. At the command *right face* all eyes turned toward the officers who had been ordering us around for the last eight weeks. That was the last we would see of them, a somewhat pleasant relief for many of us.

The ASTP group boarded the train. As usual we were packed three to a seat. I could see we were following the Mississippi River in a southerly direction.

"South? Why not North where most of us came from?"

I always thought Arkansas was far south enough.

Someone said, "I hope they won't send us to Texas!" I'm sure that must have come from a Maine boy.

An hour later the trained slowed.

"One hour's ride! The shortest one yet."

"What did that station sign say?"

"Baton Rouge!"

"That's in Louisiana, isn't it?"

A sergeant met us as we got off the train. "Fall In! Your bags will come along later." (Our duffel bags had our names on them so there was no way to lose track of them. They followed us all the way across Europe.)

We were loaded into an army truck and rode a few short miles. From what I could see out the back of the closed-in truck it looked exactly like a college campus.

"All right," barked the sergeant's voice, "You're at Louisiana State University. This is called a *star unit* of ASTP. You will be staying here for one month participating in further testing assignments and then be assigned to one of the areas of study."

All I could think was, "Wow! I'll be able to sleep in a real bed and have real showers and good college food!"

Then I noticed our truck had stopped by a football stadium, and the sergeant said, "This is where you will be bunked for the month. Under the bleachers there are hammocks, which will be your beds while you stay here. Your meals will be brought here three times a day, so make sure you have your mess kits with you. You will be under full command while you are here. You will be taking further exams and in between those you will be running the obstacle course." Further orders from the sergeant, "Evenings between seven and nine you will be escorted to various places of interest." The final order, "There will be no *fraternizing* with any of the college students here on campus." The one thing we truly learned in basic was to obey the command of superior officers. Forget about having your own ideas for fun.

The ASTP program was basically an accelerated degree program. It could be completed in two years instead of the usual four years. They placed you in a program of study, either engineering, pre-med, dentistry, mechanics, or a foreign language. During our month at the University of Louisiana they screened us to determine the best fit for our studies, and then we were sent off to a designated college somewhere.

Aside from testing, we spent much of our time on the obstacle course. I thought the calisthenics we did twice a day for 30 minutes at Camp Robinson was tiring and wearing. They barely approached the effect of the obstacle course we did at Louisiana State. We had to climb ropes and swing out over the water. We shimmied down a 20-foot wall, supposedly to get us in shape for embarking off the side of a ship in water. We carried another soldier in a fireman's carry 100 feet. We ran a 500-foot course around the football field three times wearing a full field pack, plus a few other minor feats. There was one special course I couldn't imagine why we had to do; we had to run across a 30-foot platform that was rocking and rolling all of the time. I wondered if they were training us to avoid shells landing all around. We did the obstacle course three times a day! All this in the heat of Louisiana in July!

Even though the conditions were not exactly tourist attractions, I visited many places I might never have had the opportunity to do so

Paul at Rutgers University, 1943

during my time in training with the Army. One of our evening trips took us into New Orleans and the French Quarter, albeit most of it was seen from the rear end of an Army truck with 20 other companions.

Before we knew it, the end of the month had come and we were back on the train!

"Where are we going?"

"You'll know when you get there."

At last we seemed to be going north. It was only a three-day journey, with several layovers. We changed trains three times, but we kept going north and then headed east. I always followed the sun. I recall a certain amount of excitement in my train car.

"We just entered New Jersey."

"Maybe we are going up to Massachusetts."

"Or even Maine! Wouldn't that be something?"

"We're stopping!"

"The station sign says, *New Brunswick*. The only New Brunswick I knew of was in Canada, where my dad came from, but we were still in New Jersey.

The sergeant came into our car as the train was stopping. "Now listen. You have been assigned to Rutgers University. When the train

Our ASTP cohort eating in the Rutgers Dining Hall, 1943

stops you will form outside and transportation will take you to your dormitory where you will spend the next two years in your field of study, which will be engineering." That was the first we had heard what field of study we would be placed in. The Army has a unique way of surprising you. We learned not to be sure of anything until it happened.

Rutgers University was a beautiful place, lovely shade trees; old fancy buildings and beautifully kept lawns and walkways, quite different from Camp Robinson. The campus was situated on the historic Raritan River of the Revolutionary War days. We soon learned New Jersey mosquitoes are big enough they can be mistaken for Maine seagulls at times.

One of the exciting things about being in the Army was that you could never exactly predict what your future would be like. Here I was at a wonderful university in the north, living in a clean dormitory, sleeping in a real bed. I no longer had to share a public shower with 60 other guys (You soon learn to give up a sense of modesty in the Army.) I could use a personal shower in the hall just around the corner. We had two years of extensive study ahead of us. It looked like we would hopefully miss out on the bloodiest part of the war, but things could change.

Paul in front of the governor's mansion,
Little Rock, Arkansas, 1943

Our accommodations were not exactly as I hoped they might be. We were housed in a fine dormitory, but they squeezed four of us into rooms meant for two. The special shower room was four floors down and no elevator. Going back to college was somewhat different from the experience most of us had been drafted out of just eight weeks before.

We were still in the Army. We wore our class-A uniforms, and our shoes had to have a glossy polish just like they did during basic. We still awoke to the bugle playing Reveille. We had to march to classes. We had to do this, and we had to do that. But we immediately started in classes.

It was exciting and classes were stiff. We had activity from six in the morning until eleven at night with classes from eight until five-thirty, and compulsory study hours from seven until eleven every night. They really poured it on us, but it was good.

New Brunswick looked like a nice small city to spend some free time. The railroad station was only a hop away, and in less than an hour we could be in New York City where everything was going full swing. The best part was that I was not far from home. From New York I could easily reach Boston and then Portland, Maine.

I only made $21 a month so I didn't have much money to spare. I had just enough money to get to New York City. Once I got there I didn't have much left, but that's where the USO came in. I went to Penn Station and got free donuts and coffee and free tickets to big theatres. You could get a cot to sleep on in an old abandoned hotel for 50 cents a night. So $21 went quite a ways because I didn't have much to spend it on.

After only nine months of schooling our stay at Rutgers University was suddenly halted. The United States was preparing for a big invasion of Europe. The Army didn't need us to become officers anymore. They needed regular fighters, and they needed them in great quantity.

The end of ASTP surely was a disappointment. Goodbye Rutgers University. Goodbye comfortable beds, warm dry living quarters, clean clothes, regular meals, hot showers, and beautiful surroundings.

I had a one-week furlough at home and said another good-bye to Marm and Dad. Then I boarded another crowded troop train going west for four days to "you'll know when you get there."

We arrived in Little Rock, Colorado at Camp Carson for two months of combat maneuver training, primarily amphibious and night attacks. There thousands of us *college boys*, as the regulars called us, now found ourselves assigned to the 104th Infantry Division, known as the Timberwolves.

Everything has its good side. In Colorado we had a few opportunities to do some exploring: Pikes Peak, two beautiful caverns, the Royal Gorge of the Arkansas River, colorful Redstone Park, and it was all paid for by Uncle Sam.

Two months later we were headed back east, stopping for a few days at Camp Kilmer, New Jersey before starting off on our cruise across the Atlantic.

Across the Atlantic

In the middle of the darkest night in Hoboken, New Jersey I walked up a dimly lit gangplank and boarded a ship headed across the Atlantic. Though there were hundreds of men on that boat I recall the silence. We knew this was no vacation cruise. We were finally headed for real combat.

We walked down a companionway, a narrow passageway just wide enough for an average person, to the inside of the ship. There we waited in the dark until assigned a hammock in the guts of the ship and told to try and get some sleep. The ship was still docked. There was nothing else to do but sleep. The hammocks were strung three high, and I struggled to get into my hammock on top. As I lay among the hundreds of other men I thought this must be how a bumblebee feels as it sleeps in its hive.

I awakened to the roaring sounds of a big ship at sea and instantly felt the motion that told me that we were no longer sitting quietly at a dock in New Jersey. We were ordered to get moving. As our large group slowly moved up the companionway I saw a sign over the doorway, *Achtung*. I asked what it meant.

Some smart guy answered, "Duck, or bang your head."

Later I learned it was the German word for *attention*, which in this case meant *Duck, or bang your head!* There were other signs around the boat in German, and I wondered why. Someone later told me our ship had previously been a German escort ship for the large German battleship, the Admiral Graf Spee, which was scuttled by the British in Uruguay. They sold the escort ship to the United States and it was turned into a troop ship. It seemed a bit strange to me that I should be headed into combat to fight the Germans in one of their own ships.

Up on deck I could plainly see the ship was moving. We were far at sea on the northern Atlantic with no sight of land at all, but we were not alone, for in every direction I could see many ships of all shapes and sizes. This was a convoy of ships.

It may have been daytime, but the sky was filled with dark clouds, and I could feel that the Atlantic was not a calm ocean. This was not the ocean I had known and dreamt of as a boy. I had only known Casco Bay in Portland. I used to daydream of sailing with the great explorers, Columbus, Magellan, and Captain Cook. I had once hoped to join the Navy, but as I watched in amazement at the stormy Atlantic Ocean I was quite happy I had not joined the Navy.

I heard a deep thunderous sound. A huge ship poked its nose right between us and another ship, and it looked to me like it would not fit. The fast-moving ship did not slow down but kept moving rapidly on its way. Some of its waves reached the height of our deck before it passed on through. Our sergeant explained it was a Navy destroyer looking for a German U-boat that had been detected in our area. He comforted us saying there were several such ships out there and we should always be ready to leave the ship if a torpedo hits us.

Not surprisingly, the very next activity was a lifeboat drill. I looked around at the available lifeboats and there did not seem to be anywhere near enough lifeboats to carry all of us. That was my first inclination that I was in a *combat zone*, and that I would remain close to danger until I went home, if I ever made it home.

After five slow days at sea our ship came to a stop in the darkness of night. We didn't know what to expect, but we soon walked down a gangplank with only our packs on our backs. (They told us our duffle bags would catch up with us later. Later turned out to be nearly a month.)

We arrived a few days after D-Day, and there seemed to be an uneasy quietness surrounding us. We boarded trucks, 30 men to a truck with packs, rifles and all, and began moving, towards what we did not know. Our sergeant told us we would be in *reserve* until called into action, which could be only an hour or a day, or even longer. It didn't mean we were in a safe zone only that we did not have to force our way forward toward the enemy.

The trucks finally stopped and left us in the dark. I could hear sounds of shelling in the distance. We waited together in the stillness. Even during the five-day journey across the sea we had made little conversation. As we prepared for whatever was ahead of us we didn't talk about it. What could one say really? Talk about the weather? Maybe gripe about the food. There wasn't anything pleasant to say. We were all trying hard not to acknowledge our feelings of fear. Regardless of how close or far we were from danger, there was always an underlying feeling that sooner or later our time might end.

The Medic's Armband

I had originally been trained only as a rifleman. A month before we headed for combat my platoon captain put out a call for someone to volunteer to serve as a combat aid man because there were not enough to fill the need. I gave that request a good deal of thought. As a rifleman I worried whether or not I would be able to kill another human. Here was an opportunity for me to save men's lives instead of taking them. Though any wise soldier well knew the saying, "you should never volunteer for any thing in the Army," I offered my services.

We were told we would be given one-month medical training and that would be sufficient for the task. My official title was *company aid man*, also known as a *combat medic*. My task was rather simple: stop the bleeding and prepare the wounded man for travel by litter-bearers.

My job required me to follow my platoon as closely as I could. Very often, as we approached our target the machine guns or the shells would wound one or more of my men. I had to get to the wounded man as fast as I could, even though at times there would be more than one to attend to. Many times this required getting out of my *safe* location, climbing out of my foxhole during heavy shelling, into no-man's land, to help one of my men.

I would try to find his wounds, pour sulfur powder into the wound as a disinfectant, and try to stop the bleeding, which meant simply wrapping a bandage or even two or three over the wound as fast and securely as I could. I might apply a tourniquet if necessary or rig up a splint if the bones seemed too badly out of line. If his leg needed a splint, I'd used his rifle and wrap it securely around his damaged leg. For an arm splint, I used his bayonet. Then I'd leave and catch up with the rest of the platoon. Even worse, most of our attacks were at night, and I was often fearfully confused as to where I was to go next. There were many times when I felt very much alone in this war.

Paul wearing his medic armband, 1945

I had a job to do, and I always kept that heavily on my mind. The very little medical training I had certainly did not prepare me for facing the agony and the intense pain of the soldiers I was tending to. Some of the wounds were not too bad, but others were indescribable. All I could do was, as we medics often said, "Stop the bleeding, give them a shot of morphine, and move on." (Though we did not have morphine until near the end of the war.) The hardest part was leaving a guy behind when I wasn't even sure I had done the job properly. *Patch them up* exactly describes all I could do.

If I could stop their bleeding they would have a much better chance of staying alive. Sometimes they had to wait hours before the litter-bearers found them. Then the litter-bearers might have to carry them back a mile or more. After that they were sent by ambulance to a field hospital. It could be several hours before a wounded man saw a real doctor.

I have to admit I felt inadequate for the position. My first encounter with death came at Normandy. During our first night the shelling was pretty heavy and I tried to keep up with the guys in my platoon. I came upon my first wounded man. I was trying to see where he was hit and was turning him over to find his worst wounds when my platoon sergeant said, "Doc, he's dead!" I have to admit I was pretty dumb and had very little training as a medic, especially with dead folk. From there on I was smart enough to make sure my wounded pal was still alive. The dead, I had to leave for the grave collectors who would be coming along when the shelling cooled off. For the wounded, I did all I could to keep them alive.

For the first time in history, during World War II soldiers had access to drugs such as sulfanilamide and penicillin and even better bandage materials. With these advances the combat medic could save more lives.

During training many soldiers mildly despised the medics, who were often conscientious objectors. They often ridiculed them, sometimes calling them *pill-pushers* or worse. But during the war the riflemen loved, respected and admired their medic. They needed me in combat. I would hear their loud shout or sometimes even a scream, "Doc" or "Medic!" During our rests they usually offered me the first cup of fresh coffee. I was only 19 years old, but I was often treated as if I was the most important part of their platoon.

Even though I was the lone medic, I was not treated as a stranger in my platoon of riflemen and heavy-weapons men, who carried the bazookas and such. Everyone was a comrade. I ate, slept, laughed, and sometimes even cried with my comrades. We became a family of 40 men. But it is the aid man who must stay behind with the dying friend and holds a dead man in his arms. I learned not to become too close, because the pain is too deep.

I never considered myself a brave man. There wasn't a moment when I wasn't scared, but I had to learn to live with my fears. I had to remove every emotion in my body or end up a raving madman. I had to learn to control my fears because there were others who depended on my ability to save their lives. I'm glad I did not heed that old Army saying, "Never volunteer." I'm glad I volunteered to do what I could to help save lives.

My memory from this time is filled with many blank spaces. Yet I clearly recall the deafening sound of artillery shells, loud, but eerie, the sky-filled with smoke and fire. Artillery shells make a horrendous sound the minute they leave the barrel of the gun, and they continue the sound until they hit something. I could hear them coming closer and closer until they slammed into the ground very near me. I soon learned to distinguish which side, the Germans' or ours, the shells were coming from based on where the sound moved.

The safest place was deep in the ground. It was important to know how to dig a foxhole, something we'd learned in basic. I'd get my body as low as I could, and my head almost buried in the mud or wet snow. Still, I often felt rocks and gravel coming down on me. We might lie there for some indefinable length of time. When there was a lull, we leapt out of our foxholes and followed the sergeant as fast as we could.

Our attacks were usually at night, which made it difficult to see where we were going. All I could do was to follow the guys in my platoon as closely as I could.

First, our artillery prepared the way for our attack by sending out shells. We usually aimed our attacks toward a village or a factory. In Holland, our first obstacle usually was a dike, behind which the Germans had their artillery, machine-gun stations and tanks. We had to keep moving, even as daylight came upon us.

One time as we were approaching a Belgian village we crossed a field of sugar beets in full bloom. Darkness started to cover the land and we began our attack, spreading out across the field, but we were surrounded. All hell broke loose, as we used to say, and we hit the dirt immediately as we heard the nerve-shaking sounds of machine gun fire rattle all around us from three German machine-gun nests hiding in the field. (By then I had learned a German machine gun makes a different sound than an American one.)

All night I lay in that field with my face buried in sugar beets. Every time anyone raised their head the machine guns reared up again. We called for supporting canon fire, but they were not ready for this sort of thing so it seemed like a very long time to be breathing sugar beets. Finally, a group of our boys got close enough to toss a few grenades onto the machine guns and we got out of there just as the sky was brightened by daylight.

A few days before my 19th birthday in late November 1944 we attacked a German village close to the Rhine River. We began the attack just a few hours before darkness set in. All seemed strangely quiet with only a few German mortar shells holding us back a bit. My platoon had somehow gained entrance to a few remaining houses.

I heard my platoon sergeant shouting, "Doc, over here."

I crawled out of my pile of brick cover and went to him. I could hear someone screaming in pain and the sergeant pointed him out to me. Two of our guys had been hit and were lying in the remains of the town square. I knew what I had to do.

As a combat medic I wore a small arm band with a white background with a red cross emblazed on it around one of my upper arms, not easily seen on a dark night. It was supposed to protect me from being fired upon, according to the Geneva Convention. I often thought the little armband was too small to be noticed by the enemy, unless they were right there beside me. This was my first test to see if they'd see it and honor the rules.

I started to crawl across the square, holding my armband as high as I could. The two men were bleeding badly. I knew I had to stand up to get at my bandages and work on the men. I knew there was only one way I could get at least one of my guys back to some degree of safety and that was to carry him. Three of my men were still hugging the ground nearby; they didn't seem to be wounded. I heaved one of the wounded men up on my back in a fireman's carry and started back. Then I told the rest to bring the other guy and come with me.

For some reason, known only to God, there was no machine gun firing. The other three guys started crawling and dragging the other wounded one. We all made it to safety.

For the first time I had some respect for the Geneva Convention. I did not tempt it again as openly as the first time, and I was amazed the Germans manning those machine guns recognized my very small armband and honored the rules, but I am glad they did.

Touring Europe

As a boy, I dreamed of traveling the world to see beautiful cities and lovely farms, to see the way people live. When I got my first geography book in sixth grade, I loved reading about all the far off countries of the world. I made a goal to visit all of those places someday. It seemed at the time more of a dream than a possibility.

When America joined the war in 1941 the government came out with all sorts of propaganda. I remember the famous poster on billboards across the country of Uncle Sam pointing his finger, which no matter what angle you looked at it his finger was always pointing directly at you. At the bottom the large caption read, "Uncle Sam wants you." It made me feel guilty for not signing up to fight, even before I was old enough to join.

The war certainly offered a soldier many opportunities to travel, a chance to see the world for free. I accepted this free offer. I did it willingly, but not happily.

My vision of Europe was formed very much from my childhood geography lessons and also from the movies that showed knights, castles, beautiful horses, handsome men, and beautiful women. These scenes always struck my imagination. When I look back at my visits to France, Belgium, Holland and Germany with the Army, I do not think of the exceptional beauty of those countries, but rather my mind recalls only the horrible destruction I saw of the places I had once dreamed of as a boy.

Soon after we landed at Normandy I saw the near total destruction of town after town, the castles, farms, and families. Often the only people left were elderly folk who would not leave, even as the war brought horror to their doorsteps.

Yet, there were times when I glimpsed beauty beneath the rumble. In Paris, I saw the Sacred Heart Cathedral and the Eiffel Tower. I could not go up in that sky-reaching structure because it was off limits all during the war. I had a one-night pass into the city, but I could not see much because of the blackout rule, which meant that all the lights had to be off as dark settled in.

Aachen, Germany, 1944

I saw the "dark side" of Paris that night. As I wound my way back to the hotel, prostitutes approached me on four different occasions. They each grabbed my sleeve, put a flashlight in my face and said, "You come to hotel with me. $2." I didn't even have $2. When the fourth one approached me, I was scared, but I grabbed the flashlight and put it directly in her face. She was probably 70 years old, gray-haired and wrinkled. I pushed her away and ran in the dark back to my hotel.

There were a number of nights I slept on the floor of remarkable buildings across Europe. I spent a night on the floor of Notre Dame de Reims Cathedral, an ancient structure where many French Kings were crowned.

I vividly recall the time I slept on the floor of the beautiful Cathedral of Cologne in Germany. My outfit had just taken the city of Cologne, and the Cathedral was about the only building left standing when we arrived. Bombs had damaged a small portion of the Cathedral, but for the most part it was still untouched. The rest of that ancient city built by Romans had not fared so well; over 70 percent was a mass of ruins, including all the bridges over the Rhine.

While we rested in Cologne the Army arranged for a philharmonic orchestra to perform in the cathedral in honor of those of us who had taken the city. None other than famous Andre Kostelanetz conducted, while his wife Lily Pons, a fantastic soprano, sang for us. Only days before we had been fighting the Germans in their last stand for the city, and now I had a front row *seat* on the floor for a philharmonic orchestra performance, something I had never seen or heard before. To think, I had to go to war for such a performance! Afterwards I had the privilege of shaking the hand of Lily Pons. I also shook Andre Kostelantz's hand, but somehow that didn't have the same effect.

I remember the city of Aachen, the first city in Germany we captured. Aachen had once been a great city. Long ago Charlemagne claimed it as his favored residence, and many German kings had been crowned there. Our bombs and shells left little one might recognize as the once beautiful historical city.[1]

In a little German village I remember a restless night we spent in an ancient castle. All night I listened to the sounds of shelling and kept watch as the walls and ceilings crumbled down around us. The noise made it impossible for me to sleep, though I remember hearing some of my roommates snoring. We approached the castle under darkness and had not had a chance to see it well in the light. In the morning we saw the walls were lined with beautifully-painted portraits, I assume of the German owners of the castle. Some of our boys found great delight in throwing bayonets at the portraits. That sort of hate bothered me, but I understood how they felt.

Giant bridges fascinate me. However, the quickest way to slow down your enemy in war is to destroy their bridges. This was done all over Europe, but especially along the Rhine. The Rhine River is the largest river in Europe, beginning high in the mountains of Switzerland and ending in the lovely city of Amsterdam. I later traveled up and

---

1   I have since returned to both Aachen and Cologne, and was amazed by how the Germans have restored their cities to historical conditions.

down that gorgeous river, taking in the views of the uncountable castles and the far-reaching vineyards. During the war Allied bombers destroyed nearly all of the Rhine bridges, which helped us drive the Germans back, but also created a challenge for us to find a way to get across the river to pursue them.

After we took Cologne news came that our side had captured a bridge to the south in Remagen. We heard the bridge was still intact to a certain extent. The goal was to get as many of our forces across the bridge as possible before it fell into the Rhine. Every vehicle we had at our disposal was loaded with troops and equipment. My ride that day was a Weasel, a small vehicle that could operate both on land and in water. Our whole division of 15,000 men travelled along a bomb-damaged highway, through the great city of Bonn and other towns and cities along the way, and eventually to Remagen.

When we arrived, the bridge didn't look very stable to me. Across the river were high hills. I could just imagine the Germans hiding up there with their guns waiting for us to cross so they might shower us and wipe out our entire division. The vehicles crossed in a slow parade. We waited over an hour for our turn to cross. Except for the grinding of engines it was amazingly quiet. If the bridge did not hold I feared I'd be swimming in the Rhine. We learned later that shortly after our crossing the bridge did indeed collapse, putting an end to the crossing for more of our troops.

Winter was then upon us but that did not slow us down. We continued to fight from village to village, destroying them as we moved along. Villages seemed to be a last bastion of defense for the Germans as we kept pushing them back. Aside from the German soldiers, the villages seemed deserted. I assume the civilians had all been evacuated.

Most of the houses in Germany were made of brick. The streets were lined with brick structures on both sides, all connected together, with front entrances, and usually gardens in the back. The German soldiers made their last stands in what was left of the brick homes. The only way we could approach was to kick the door open and toss

Paul (far left with umbrella) riding in a Weasel, May, 1945

in a few hand grenades. That usually made it impossible for any more Germans to hide therein. Our usual problem was that German tanks were always stationed at the upper end of each street and were just waiting for us to attack in the open street. Our own tanks often had the task of facing the German tanks head on. This kind of fighting often left nearly nothing of the town.

Every city in the line of fire was in ruins; this is how war has always been throughout history. It was difficult for me to see the destruction of buildings and bridges, but seeing how this war destroyed the lives of so many millions of people was what truly ached in my heart. I saw people sitting beside a road or a building with their broken suitcases or just boxes and bags. I saw them slowly walking along a road as if they knew not where they were going.

As we fought our way through Holland I saw an elderly couple standing on the edge of what was left of their farm, most of the buildings destroyed. Tanks and heavy artillery guns had torn up their fields and the cattle all lay belly-up. The couple looked at what was left of their lives. They had spent their lives building a life on their farm and it was destroyed. All I could think of was my own grandparents and their lovely farm in northern Maine. This couple was looking at the ruins of their life's work.

One thing I missed during my year and a half in battle was the presence of children. There were so few of them because many had been sent away to safety, but sometimes during moments of peacetime I would see children come from out of the ruins. They were always standing by whenever our company kitchen caught up with us and we had a real meal. When we cleaned our mess kits we did not dump the remains in a trash can but shared it with the many kids waiting around. I am sure most of us made sure that we had plenty left in our mess kits.

Images of those hungry children, the farm couple, the buildings in ruins, and all the lost souls we encountered along the way still linger in my mind. War is the mass destruction of humanity. Those images and the feelings they stir up inside me never seem to leave.

Good Memories

In the combat zones of Europe I was exposed to the sight of a lot of killing and wounding of men and the massive destruction of homes, farms, cathedrals, bridges, and on and on. I do not wish to remember much of what I saw. When I returned home the best way to get over the war was to put those kinds of memories far back in my memory library. However, I have always kept alive a few good memories that warmed my Maine boy heart in those dark days of war.

The first one occurred in Holland. Our task in Holland was to cut off the Port of Antwerp in Belgium, meaning we had to encircle the area and push the Germans out of Holland. Our battles moved from one dike to another, shelling and bombing everything they might use as a barricade, which could be bridges, farms, even whole towns. It bothered me to see those beautiful farm buildings destroyed, and even worse was seeing hundreds of beautiful cattle lying belly up in the fields as we pushed our way over them.

Our platoon had been pushing hard for three days, and finally we came to rest at a half-destroyed barn. We knew there must be some hay inside, which would give us a dry comfortable place to get a bit of rest out of the wetness typical of Holland. We bedded down after a meal of a K-Rations, and were trying to sleep, when suddenly, just outside the barn, came am intensive blatting sound. I immediately knew what it was.

One of our New York City men shouted, "What in hell is that?"

I said, "Those are cows coming to be milked."

"Yeah," was his answer, "and how are we going to get milk from them?"

My answer, as any Maine farm boy would say, "I can milk them, and I'll go right out and do that." I took off my metal helmet and soon filled it with fresh milk. I filled it three times, giving all my guys a chance to have a taste of fresh milk. There's nothing like a warm glass of fresh milk to put anyone to sleep immediately. Indeed, we slept well that night, something we'd been deprived of for many days.

Another happy memory happened in the town of Inden, Germany. We had been attacking the town for two days, going from house to house, or what was left of them, lots of shelling from both sides, and German tanks covering every entry along the streets. The Germans began a heavy bombardment. Tanks barreled up the streets. Our platoon leader called for our artillery, and the only place we could find to hide in safety was a cellar in the remains of a house. Night came and everything seemed to come to a halt, but as soon as we tried to get a bit of sleep it all started over again.

This kept up, off and on, for the next three days, while we were holed up in this cellar waiting for the word to move. We soon ate all our rations and on the third night we ran out of food. We tried to sleep when we heard a "honk, honk" outside. I knew exactly what it was, as my grandfather always kept several geese at the farm. Once again, the loudmouth yelled for someone to, "Shoot those—geese!"

I thought of a better idea. I grabbed a helper and we went out in the dark. We carefully approached one of the geese and got hold of it. My friend wanted to shoot it, but I remembered how my grandfather took the life of his geese, by simply wringing their necks, which is what I did.

Jumping back into our cellar hole we pulled off all the feathers. I took out my medical scissors and cut up the bird into small pieces. The next thing we had to figure out was how to cook it. Our platoon sergeant always carried a small Bunsen burner, and soon we had it going. Before very long each of us had a few small pieces of a very delicious goose. We moved out of the cellar the next day, still under heavy shelling, but the goose must have helped us on our way because we made a safe exit.

Even in war, life goes on. I learned this on another occasion when we were holed up in a German village waiting for orders to move or attack. We had just found a place to sit and wait in the basement of an apartment building. I heard what sounded like a woman screaming coming from one of the connecting cellars. I got one of my platoon mates to go with me and we soon located the source of the screams. There was a woman lying on the brick floor with an older woman standing beside her. I soon realized the younger woman was giving birth. I wondered why they were still in the village while it was under so much firing; I suppose the young woman had not been in any condition to move. The older woman stood there and did not seem to be doing anything to help the young mother, so I approached showing my medics badge on my arm, and she stepped aside.

The baby was pretty well along its way. I got hold of what I could of it and gave it a pull. Much to my surprise, out it came, blood and all. It was so dark in there, I don't even recall if it was a boy or a girl. I knew I had to cut the umbilical cord, just as my grandfather and I had done for the calves on the farm in Maine, so I took out my medical scissors and cut it apart. Fortunately at that time I had just gotten my musette bags filled again with bandages. Using a good supply of the fresh bandages, I soon had both mother and baby taken care of. I didn't know if I had done the right thing or not, but the older woman looked at me with tears in her eyes, with a look that told me *thank you*.

Christmas 1944

We hardly saw any dry days in Holland, where we endured a month in the Battle of the Dykes. We were continually wet, and so were our clothes, boots, and socks. An alarming number of our men suffered from trench foot, a terrifying illness named from the days of World War I when troops lived and fought in trenches. To ward it off some men carried spare socks under their shirts to keep them dry, but it was nearly impossible as we slept in watery foxholes.

A foxhole is often the only place to catch a few winks in open territory pinned down by enemy fire. I don't know why they call it a foxhole. I doubt a well-adjusted fox would even look at such a place—merely a shallow hole. In basic we were told it ought to be at least 12 inches deep, wide enough to curl up in and long enough to fit your body. We each dug our own hole with a small spade we kept in our packs.

I found foxholes could be relatively comfortable, depending where I dug. In France and Belgium the soil is relatively good for farming, which made it easy to dig. In Holland, however, the sea is only about 12 inches below the surface. It was easy enough to dig a hole in the muddy topsoil, but if I dug more than a foot deep seawater would seep in and soon I was sleeping in a very uncomfortable wet bed.

We fought our way across France, Belgium, Holland, and into Germany. We had come so far it seemed there was no stopping us from going all the way to the Rhine River by Christmastime. In November, we came against the Siegfried Line, a massive bastion of fortresses, gun mounts, and tank traps and other obstacles extending nearly 400 miles along the western border of Germany. If we could just burst through that seemingly impregnable line we would have the Germans on the run.

We almost made it through when the unbelievable happened, the Battle of the Bulge, Germany's infamous last-ditch attempt, stopped us immediately. On December 16th we had to turn away from the Rhine to stop the German forces coming north in our direction.

As Christmas neared we entered the remains of Lamersdorf, a small German village and found relative safety as we waited for the command to move on. Every night our platoon went out on combat patrol in search of German soldiers. While we were still on the northern front of the Battle of the Bulge there was very little combative activity. German forces had slowed down quite a lot.

Everything seemed quiet, almost eerie. No explosives or dangerous activity. I kept expecting to hear the whining of shells coming in our direction. I kept my helmet close at hand, though it was a relief to get it off my head for a while. It almost seemed as though the war was over.

Much of the village had been destroyed during the days before we settled in. There were practically no fully-erected buildings and the few left had been taken over by the brass (officers). My close companion Len and I found a wonderful cellar in the village. It provided a warm dry place to hang our helmets and medical bags, which by now had very few bandages left.

Leonard Broughman (Len) was from North Carolina. Since I was a New England boy we had many great discussions as to who rightfully won the Civil War. We were both combat medics. He was with another platoon. Whenever there was a break we would get together and share our packages from home. Len had a good singing voice. We loved to sing hymns and popular songs together.

Wonderful things began to happen while we waited in Lamersdorf. We were not going on any attacks. Only a few shells exploded in the village from German artillery. It almost became natural to sleep at night, instead of waiting for the next move to attack. Sometimes I even slept all night long. The real blessing—three meals a day right out of a regular military kitchen. Because of the lull, field kitchens could move right up to the front and cook real meals. After eating only K-rations for over two months this was a real pleasure.

Christmas came in many different packages. Yes, packages! Military mail service is not like the post office. Mail comes up through the rear agencies. I don't know how it was done, but I marvel at the efficiency of it when I remember the uncountable military outfits all over Europe, and yet our mail eventually found us.

Paul (right) and friend playing pinochle at Christmas time in a bombed-out cellar in Lamersdorf

That Christmas, Santa Claus arrived in many forms. Mail call was perhaps the happiest time of all. Packages were filled with cookies, candies, cigarettes, tobacco, and just about anything you can imagine. I even found toilet paper in one of my packages. What a gift! And letters! Letters from our mothers, our sisters, our girlfriends. (I didn't have a girlfriend, but I had four sisters!) I even got letters from Dad, who probably hadn't written any letters since he courted Mom. His letters were especially meaningful to me.

Picture Len and me at our *Christmas residence*. We found a small wood stove and used the bashed-up furniture and building materials for fuel. We hoped to find a Christmas tree. Germany has excellent fir trees, just beautiful for Christmas, but the shelling had completely demolished the trees. Len and I made decorations and managed to create a makeshift tree out of our Christmas packaging materials and some of the items we found around in the rubble.

Len had a strong tenor voice, and I could sing just about anything. Soon we were trying to sing all of the Christmas carols we could remember. Before we knew it, several of our neighbors (guys in nearby cellars) heard us and joined in. Soon we had a good choral group going. All was merry in our humble abode until our platoon sergeant stepped in.

The quiet look on his face told us something was going to change. He waited till we finished the carol. "Get some sleep, guys. We're going out on patrol at 0300. That's three a.m. for you non-military folk. I won't tell you what the rest of Christmas 1944 was like and spoil your vision of our *Merry Christmas*.

Sneak Patrol to the Russians

We thought the war in Europe was over. No more midnight patrols seeking Germans. No more shelling. Germany had not officially surrendered, but we knew they were close to doing so. We had been ordered to stop advancing. Large numbers of German soldiers were coming to us to surrender because the Russians were on their tails, and no German wanted to be captured by the Russians.

Since the war was pretty much over, I was enjoying the quiet and calm when my platoon sergeant called me out of my cellar. Our battalion commander had always been a *pusher*, meaning that he and his men always achieved their goals in high fashion. He asked if I would go on a sneak patrol to meet the Russians.

The first words out of my mouth, "You've got to be kidding! Why me?"

He explained that all the other men were needed for the mission, a platoon lieutenant to be the leader, a sergeant who could speak German, a corporal who could speak some Russian, and a staff sergeant to be second in charge. The only problem was they could not find an aid man to volunteer. I don't know why our captain wanted to do this, but I think he wanted his men to be the first to make contact with the Russians.

I immediately thought of the Army adage, "Never volunteer for anything." I had always stuck quite well to that saying (except for the one time I volunteered to be a combat medic, but I did that because I wanted to save lives instead of take them). I could not come up with a good reason to join the sneak patrol mission. Then I thought of the roads I've taken in life and how the "less traveled" paths have often led me just where I needed to be. I accepted the call to join the sneak patrol because I felt *called* to it. Partly, I felt I really was needed, and if I didn't volunteer the mission could not be carried out.

Lieutenant Bob Bartlett gathered his patrol together the evening before departure. He had a map of the area, which showed a few small German towns along our way. His plan was to take open roads as much as we could, knowing the Germans wanted to surrender to us rather

Meeting the Russians, Paul fifth from the left, April 32, 1945

than to the Russians and hopefully they would not give us any trouble. If we were to meet with any potential struggle we were to take to the woods, which were plentiful on our route. We knew we would see hundreds of German soldiers. They had been coming to our lines for days already trying to stay out of the hands of the Russians.

We were not to carry any arms, which seemed scary at first, but our mission was not to kill or capture, only to make the connection with the Russians. We wanted the Germans to know we were on a peaceful mission. Our staff sergeant carried a small American flag, which was all we had to show who we were.

We headed out, five of us, at daylight the next morning, filled with an unexplainable feeling. Immediately we began to see German soldiers, some alone, mostly scattered in no formation with no obvious leaders, un-armed and just slowly moving in our direction. Some stopped to ask us what direction they should take to surrender. Our German-speaking man enjoyed telling them how to get there. I can still see the looks on their faces, the shabby condition of their uniforms and their boots. They had been fleeing the Russians for days, perhaps weeks. I wanted to share my rations with them, but that might not have been a wise thing to do.

We had heard the only Germans we should be cautious about at this stage were the SS, which stood for *Schultzstaffel*, meaning "protection squadron." This selective group was formed early on to protect Hitler wherever he went, but later became the most powerful of all of the German military formations. We met up with some of them as we fought across Europe.

We moved right along our route and made good time, easy as a picnic. We soon approached the edge of the first village on our map, and here we began to see civilians standing outside of the houses along the way. Apparently they had heard "the Americans are coming," not just five American soldiers carrying a small American flag. As I reflect back on this mission it seems more of a Hollywood farce than a military operation.

We came across several German men sprawled beside the road. Our German-speaker talked and found out several felt they could go no further because of severe blistering on their feet. They had been walking for many miles just to get away from the Russians and were finding it almost impossible to continue. I had plenty of bandages in my two mussette bags just in case of heavy trouble as well as ointments I always carried for foot problems. I had to use most of the bandages I'd brought for I'd never seen such badly bruised feet. My work on the Germans brought out quite a few civilians to watch. I suppose they could not believe an American soldier would help a German.

It was getting rather late in the afternoon and Lt. Bartlett asked some of the civilians if they would take us to the *burgomeisters'* house. (A burgomeister is the mayor or head magistrate in a town or village.) We were very politely welcomed into his home. He spoke fairly good English. His wife treated us with some kind of drink, which I thought was wine of some sort so I did not drink any. (I had never been accustomed to alcoholic drinks, mostly because my parents taught me that they were harmful to your health.)

We explained to the burgomeister what our mission was, and then he gave us some helpful information. We talked about the many German soldiers we had met. Some seemed to earnestly want to surrender and simply wanted to know which way to go, but others stood away from us and were not friendly. Some of them were still carrying weapons, which gave us a bit of concern. We suggested the burgomeister put out a call that all weapons should be brought to his yard and deposited there. We did not think this would happen, but to our surprise the word went out and spread fast and soon there were many following the order.

The burgomeister warned us about a company of SS troops staying on the edge of town who were Hitler's "chosen" ones who had been ordered never to give up. He also told us their commander had left town to make contact with some of his superiors, and that we should avoid them if possible.

After we shared some of our rations with him and his wife, he suggested we stay the night in his town. He had a small cottage near a pond we could all stay in. Lt. Bartlett thought it was a good idea as it was getting dark and it would soon be difficult to travel onward. As darkness fell the burgomeister led us to the cottage and we made our sleeping places on the floor. It felt so good to be able to just drop down, even on the floor, but it didn't last very long. Around four o'clock in the morning Lt. Bartlett woke us and told us to get ready to move out. He wanted to get far away from the town before the SS commander came back. Soon we were on our way moving as fast as we could in the dark.

We kept moving at a good pace and by daylight we had put a few miles between the last village and us. Then we saw someone coming on a bicycle, moving very fast. It was the burgomeister. Nearly out of breath he told us the SS commander had arrived late in the evening and he and his men would soon be looking for us. Fortunately, the SS commander did not know we had been in the cottage earlier, or that we had taken off in the night. We made a fast decision to take to the woods, and quickly thanked the burgomeister for his kindness.

Our second day was a real slow one. We followed the road as closely as we could, but always stayed in the woods for cover. Several times a small Volkswagen passed by with two SS officers and a driver. That was the only traffic on the road. We made very slow progress all day through the woods. When darkness came we simply bedded down for the night.

Lt. Bartlett checked his map and decided we were within a few miles of the last village before the river. We thought it safe enough to take to the road again and possibly we could get to the river by noon.

Our estimate was pretty close. Around noon we began to see scattered houses up ahead, and then we saw people. The closer we got, the more people we could see. As we walked down the gentle slope of the road we were shocked by what we saw. Hundreds of people sitting, standing, lying down in an open field with bags and boxes and mangled suitcases of all sorts beside them. Never had we seen such a sight.

A man saw our American flag and stepped up to us. He began talking, not in English or in German, but in Russian. Our Russian interpreter stepped forward and we soon learned all of these people were Russians who had been caught behind German lines over the years, some as slave laborers. They were all trying to get across the Elbe River and find their way back to Russia, but there were no boats, no vehicles of any sort of transportation to help them on their way. They seemed to have no food, and I thought, not very much life left. It is a scene that will never leave my mind.

Then Russian officers and enlisted men greeted us and there was lots of handshaking, even hugging and laughing, and lots of talking I could not understand. I was the only one who had a camera of any sort, just a little box camera I had picked up out of a destroyed German house earlier on. I had found some film in a destroyed shop several towns back in Germany. I took pictures of these new Russian and American friends standing together. The prints may not be much to look at now, but the memory of that meeting remains vivid in my mind.

The Russians escorted us down to the river to a small rowboat, and a Russian soldier rowed us across the Elbe River. We made it! Our strange mission accomplished, but it was not over. We still had to return to our base.

We landed on the other of side of the river and looked in disbelief at the sight of an American jeep with several Russian men standing beside it. (I imagine the American jeep must have been one of our

American lend-lease gifts to Russia.). We loaded into the over-crowded jeep and headed away from the river.

We arrived at a fancy estate with a lovely mansion, barns, out buildings, and a few Russian military vehicles parked nearby. They took us into the mansion and led us into a dining room with several elaborately dressed Russian officers seated around the table. They escorted us to five empty chairs around the table. I felt like I was a very important person—not just a private first class. They served us large glasses of what I took to be water. I had not had a good drink of water since we left; the states only chlorinated water in our canteens. I immediately took my glass and nearly emptied it down my dry throat before I realized it did not taste like water, but had a strange taste I could not identify. With two good interpreters available Lt. Bartlett and the Russian officers began chattering. I don't remember much more as things began to get quite fuzzy. Later, I learned what I thought was water was really vodka.

We were directed to a barn to sleep, which I did promptly. Sometime in the middle of the night Lt. Bartlett woke us and told us to get ready to go. The Russians were going to take the five of us back in a German flatbed truck. It was the strangest ride. We left sometime after midnight, a strange time for any vehicle to be traveling. Driving at night was not something that had been done in Germany for quite some time, so we made quite a scene to those awakened by the sound of the truck. With headlights blazing, we drove right through the three villages we had spent days walking through. It was interesting to see many German soldiers standing beside the roads, probably stunned by the sight of us.

Lt. Bartlett asked the Russian driver to stop at the burgomeister's house, where we had stashed various souvenirs in the bushes, mostly small arms weapons (including a rare Russian revolver with a carved wooden handle I had found). We were still somewhat concerned about the German SS officer, but our stop was very short and we made off for the final lap of our journey without any trouble.

What we had not planned for was our arrival at the American line. We approached our military out-post at around three o'clock in the morning and were immediately brought to a halt by several military police, flashlights and guns aimed right at us. Since we were an unauthorized patrol no one knew of our mission, nor expected such a strange arrival. They must have been baffled to find our odd little group of English-speakers and Russian-speakers riding in a German truck. They asked us for the password, which we didn't know. They ordered us to immediately dismount and loaded us into three jeeps. They locked us in for the rest of the night. Lt. Bartlett did his best to explain. The following day the MPs were able to get in touch with our battalion commander who explained our mission, and they finally sent us back to our outfits.

There were no banners, or flags, or brass bands, or photographers welcoming us back. Almost nobody even knew we had gone. If they missed us they simply assumed we had gone to rest camp.

We believed, and I still do, we were the first Americans to make contact with the Russian army. We had no way of making it an official event because we had no authorization to carry out such a mission, except from our battalion commander, who wasn't going to make a big fuss about it because he knew he had no authority to even plan such an event. The next day we learned a unit from the 69th Division, along with several honored dignitaries, had made an authorized connection with the Russian army and received the honor of being the first to do so with photographs and medals to go with it. The only record of our meeting is in our division's regimental history that mentions "a sneak patrol that made contact with the Russians at about that time." [2]

---

2   Over the years I have tried to make contact with the four other men of the sneak patrol. I finally located the home of Lt. Bartlett several years ago. His wife sadly informed me he had recently died, and that he had tried in vain to find us too. I did make contact with our German interpreter, but he passed on before I could get together with him.

Buchenwald

As a boy growing up in the safety and security of rural Maine I had never seen death. I had never attended a funeral. The war changed all of that. Throughout the war I saw so many dead bodies of men, women, and even a few dead children, I became somewhat hardened to that kind of scene, until my division over-ran two concentration camps.

My platoon was among those who had driven the German SS troops out of one of their "work camps" near the village of Nordhausen. I only had a brief glimpse of the entire scene, as we were still pushing forward. It was almost more than I could deal with emotionally. The scene will never leave my memory. There were hundreds of bodies strewn and piled everywhere. We were quickly directed out of the area and told our medical attachment would very soon take over.

A few days later I was allowed, with several others from my platoon, to visit Buchenwald, which had been recently taken by another unit. There I saw wagons filled with bodies waiting to be cremated. Apparently there had been so many the Nazis did not have enough time to take care of that situation. Most of the live prisoners at Buchenwald had been taken away just before I got there, but there were still some around. They looked more like scarecrows than men and showed very little life. They just stared at us as though they couldn't even talk. Some of us tried to give them some of our rations, but we were immediately told not to do that as it might make them sick since they had not had food for quite a long time. The medical teams would soon arrive and take care of them.

The camp consisted of nearly 100 or so very long barracks. There were no toilet facilities in the barracks, only ditches outside for such use. The prisoners slept on shelf-like structures in which at least six or more men slept side by side. I understand that when one died, which was quite regularly, the body may not be moved for several days, only until the crematory was able to take the body.

The crematories were long buildings with many open ovens. Bodies were loaded onto a conveyor structure and rolled directly into the oven. The conveyors were designed to fit one body at time, but since the

Prisoner bodies at Buchenwald and Nordhausen concentration camps, 1945

bodies were so emaciated it could hold three bodies, which made it quicker to dispose of them. Near the end of the war, so many prisoners died the bodies simply were stacked waiting their turn for cremation.

We also visited a building referred to as the *hospital*, where scientific experimentation was done. Doctors injected prisoners with various chemicals and kept them in pits to observe how they reacted to the chemicals. The pits were eight feet deep, rectangular, concrete holes. Prisoners could be left there for several days during the scientific observation.

Around the grounds of camp were several structures used for punishment. They were simply two-posted frames with a wooden bar connecting the posts across the top. They bound a prisoner's hands behind him and then hung him by the hands. I cringe to think of the extent of the torture.

I have been back to Buchenwald in recent years.

When I stopped at an information place near Buchenwald I was told the former concentration camp had been made into a sort of museum. I found that hard to believe, but I followed the directions given and came upon a very fancy entrance sign instead of seeing the former headquarters of the German SS troops. Everything was quite different from what I had seen in 1945. I expected to see the barracks, but they were gone. Only flat gravel pads remained. At the end of each gravel pad plaques listed the number of prisoners who had last been housed there. The hospital was still standing. There was no sign of the observation pits. The crematory was still there.

It still confuses me to think the German people

Apparatus made to hang prisoners with their hands tied behind them.

Paul talking to a prisoner

Crematorium ovens, Buchenwald, April, 1945

would go to such lengths to retain those places of torture. The German people I have made friends with are deeply ashamed of what their country did during those dark times. So many places that were destroyed during the war have since been beautifully restored. I've enjoyed my visits to Germany and took every opportunity to make friendly contact with men who were my enemy during those trying times. I have found them all very willing to share many of the same things I have tried to explain. I even found some who were on the same battlefield. My visits to Germany since the war have helped me to realize what I already knew, that the German people are no different than we Americans.

I do not wish to relive these memories, yet I write them for anyone who wishes to try to understand what happens when an unprepared Maine boy, or American boy, or German boy must face the horrors of our world.

No Fraternizing!

Germany surrendered on May 9, 1945. My infantry division was deep in the heart of Germany, approximately 40 miles from Berlin. We found ourselves in the town of Bitterfeld, mostly known for its beer production, which sadly was out of business due to our destructive attacks across Germany.

There was nothing urgent to do anymore, and it became a good time to clean up, shave, wear a clean uniform, and polish our boots every day. (But I wanted to know, how do you polish a boot caked with mud and blood?)

There was time for a little freedom and even some touring, but there was one definite and strict order to adhere: "No fraternizing!" In other words, no personal connections between military personnel and civilians allowed.

At the time, many German civilians were returning to their homes, or what was left of their homes, many of which had been taken over by American soldiers. Some had to find neighbors or friends to reside with until their houses would be rebuilt.

The artillery had spared few of the houses in most towns, but there was very little destruction in Bitterfeld. We did not have regular beds, because there were so many of us, however we did have complete use of the houses we occupied. The backyard gardens were a wonderful place to relax among the flowers. We spent considerable time just

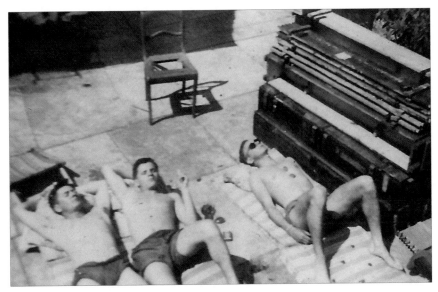

Paul and friends sunbathing, Bitterfeld, Germany, 1945

sunning ourselves and playing pinochle, which had become the favorite Army card game.

We now had lots of free time and no fear of being shelled or machine-gunned, but no fraternizing! These civilians looked just like our mothers and fathers and grandmothers and girlfriends. Many of the German civilians were still somewhat frightened by so many American military men, but some wanted to be friendly. Most of us could not speak German, though most of the Germans could converse fairly well in English.

One afternoon Len and I found our way to a local park. It was May and the place was full of flowers and trees putting on their summer leaves. It seemed like a good place to remove our shirts, out of sight from any officer who might cause us some difficulty, and we could get a good share of what we had been missing for more than a year, warm sunshine!

We were truly obeying our military order of "no fraternizing" when two young women came along and started talking to us in English. They seemed to be proud of their ability to converse in English and asked us a few questions about ourselves. I felt somewhat ill at ease because I tried very hard to obey all commands. We were very much on the alert for any officers walking by, but we hadn't seen or talked to any females for over a year. The town was over-run with American soldiers; many of whom I'm sure would have loved to be in our place.

They told us the terrible things they had lived through and said they were so glad the war was over. We did not have much time to talk because we had to report back soon. Before they left they invited us to their home near the end of the village. It was too good to turn down, so we took a chance and made a date for suppertime. The girls drew a map for us to follow.

Now it just so happened our mail had come in the day before and there was a package for me from home. I had previously v-mailed home to Marm to send me something I could cook. That day a package of ready-mix ginger bread arrived.

Before suppertime we found our way to the house at the edge of the village. Their mom was quite surprised to see us for the girls had not told her we were coming, but her welcome was as warm as it would have been from Marm if I had invited someone to our house. They had very little food to share, but the gingerbread was a big hit, and the family was warm and welcoming. It felt somewhat strange to me because just a few days before we were destroying their homes and killing their men. Our only worry was getting back to our quarters before bed check. I didn't have any guilty feelings about this escapade as I felt the fraternizing rule was absurd.

Camp Lucky Strike

VE Day Parade, Bitterfeld, Germany, May 8, 1945

One month after the war with Germany ended orders came to pack our bags.

"Where are we going?"

"You'll know when you get there!" (I hope I never hear those words again in my lifetime.)

Packing up wasn't difficult as I had very few personal items. We were issued three days of K-rations for our travels through France, where we would hopefully get on a troopship home, of course that was only rumor. We began our final march to the railroad station through the well-bombed city of Leipzig. We spent three days packed in old forty-and-eight boxcars left over from World War I (designed to carry forty men or eight horses). We finally pulled to a stop in the town of Le Havre, France, to once again see the waters of the English Channel.

Outside of the coastal city of Le Havre the Army erected a huge temporary military installation known as Camp Lucky Strike. It was a massive tent city intended to prepare thousands of military men to return home. We spent a week getting new uniforms and medical inspections, enjoying real hot showers, eating meals in the chow hall, and waking to the bugles playing Reveille each day.

I was somewhat concerned about our duffle bag inspections. I had carried that monstrosity from the time we landed until we were ready to go home. Though I did not carry it into combat, but it was always brought up whenever the fighting stopped while we were in reserve. I had to declare all I carried in my bag. I had gathered quite a few souvenirs. My loot consisted of an SS officer's dagger with the slogan *Alles Fer Deutchland* on it, meaning "all for Germany." I was quite proud of that item, as I had taken it off an SS officer when he surrendered to us. I carried a set of brass knuckles caked with dried blood that I had picked out of the mud when we over-ran Buchenwald Concentration Camp. I also had a P-38 German revolver, a Smith and Wesson Russian revolver I had taken from surrendering German soldiers while on the sneak patrol, plus a Belgian automatic revolver, a German portrait camera, and a choice Ilex camera. I hasten to say that I did not steal those items. I actually picked them up in several places where they were just laying around. I was completely surprised when the inspection officer simply recorded them and passed me on.

Near the end of two weeks we gladly marched several miles carrying those heavy duffle bags and happily walked up the gangplank to the ship that would carry us home. I felt like a kid arriving at a circus. It was such a different feeling from the time I walked up the gangplank at Hoboken, New Jersey back in 1944 on our way to Normandy.

Home from the War

Our journey home took four glorious days, all with calm sailing and noticeable lack of seasickness. It was late June and every day the sun shone warmly on us. Those days stood out for all of us because during our many days in battle, we seldom saw the sunshine, especially in Belgium, Holland and all through Germany.

We were having breakfast when they announced our approach into New York Harbor. We began to see all kinds of ships passing us on their way out, and then we saw the Statue of Liberty. The sun was bouncing off the lady's shoulders. Before we realized it, the bay was overflowing with all sorts of vessels, one of them carried a blaring fancy-uniformed band and another was loaded with beautiful gals all dressed in nothing but skimpy bathing suits. Boat after boat of all sizes and shapes kept circling around and around us. I could see a lot of guys wiping the tears from their eyes, and I have to admit tears were rapidly flowing from my eyes too.

We were going home. It is a strange feeling to have when many of us figured we probably would never go home again. It was almost overwhelming. Our boat came closer and closer to the docking place.

Our platoon sergeant called us together to give us some last words. "After we land you will be given time and fares to get home. You will all get a week furlough, and then you will report back at Camp Kilmer in New Jersey, and from there we will head for Camp San Luis Obispo, California, where we will get amphibious training for the attack on Japan."

Can you imagine the quietness of several hundred men at such a time? What could one say? Have you ever had a mean boy stick a pin in your only balloon on the Fourth of July? We thought we had won our war. We thought we would be going home, perhaps for a few weeks and then await our discharge.

The war was not over for us.

Thousands of soldiers were released into New York City all heading for the train station to reach cities across the country. It took me all of the next day to get to Portland after changing trains in Boston, along

Paul visiting his family on furlough. (back row) Sisters Ruth, Ada, and Thelma (Teddy), (front row) Paul and his brother-in-law Bill Tiffany.

with several hundred others all with the same idea. I remember a great deal of whooping and hollering all over those stations.

At 8 a.m. a day and a half after disembarking the ship, I walked proudly up Congress Street to my home on Neal Street, the same one I left in 1943. I could hardly keep from running.

Back home my mother had been waiting for four of us to return home from our wartime duties. Two of my older brothers had enlisted in the Air Force right after the Pearl Harbor attack. Mike was sent off to England, and Robert was sent off to India where he flew supplies into China over the Himalayas. Twice he had to bail out, but each time he was rescued. My sister Ruth enlisted in the Navy and served as a pharmacist mate in Alaska.

Ruth was the first to come home. She hit the call button at the foot of the stairs, and Marm knew Ruth's voice and she buzzed her in. Then Mike arrived, buzzed the apartment and said, "I'm home!" into the intercom.

Marm answered, "Oh Paul, I'm so glad."

Mike quickly replied, "No, I'm Mike."

A day or two later Bob came home, rang the buzzer, and got the same answer.

"Oh Paul, I'm, so glad you made it."

"No, Marm. I'm Bob."

Three days later I rang the buzzer, and then she knew.

That week at home was like a strange dream. It didn't seem real. I was the only one of my siblings who had to go back.

When I left home this time, I knew I would not be coming back.

I am sure Marm and Dad and even my brothers and sisters did not expect me to come back. We didn't even mention such a thing, but there were a lot of tears when my five days were over and I headed to Camp Kilmer, New Jersey.

Leaving Home Again

Just a little over a year before we had left Camp Kilmer and crossed the Atlantic Ocean to the war in Europe. This time we were at Camp Kilmer boarding a train going west heading to the war in Asia, specifically Japan. It was my third troop train ride across the same part of the country. I had a strong feeling this trip would be my last crossing ever, though I never mentioned my thoughts. I had experienced intensive war activity for over a year, attack after attack, seeing so many killed or wounded, wondering when it would be my turn. Those thoughts would not go away.

We spent five days on the troop train, once again subjected to over-packed, discarded old passenger cars, and trying to sleep on our duffle bags while jammed between six other guys. We were not a very happy bunch of GIs.

Our hearts perked up when our train made a one-hour stop in Nebraska and we were treated to the hospitality of the volunteers of the North Platte Canteen. Practically all troop trains traveling across the country went through North Platte at the time, and swarms of wonderful warm-hearted folk provided all sorts of pies, cookies, and sandwiches to them. Ask any serviceperson who crossed the country by troop train during the war and they will all tell you the same story. It was the highlight of our trip and helped to make life worth living after the horrors we had experienced in Europe.

Once we were back on the train the men fell back into quietness. We had seen enough of war and here we were headed for more of it. We had given our best. I am sure no one felt like a hero. We were no longer young boys, full of fun and games. War seems to age a person faster. One more day and we would be at Camp San Luis Obispo for advanced amphibious training. I wasn't quite sure what that meant, but I was not looking forward to it.

Morning came, and we heard the usual loud voice of the sergeant, "Now listen to this!" Yet, his message wasn't quite the same as usual, "The Japs have surrendered!"

We didn't say a word.

Someone finally said, "Aw, come on, don't give us that shit!"

None of us believed the sergeant; we just thought he was trying to be funny. There was an odd silence for just a brief moment, and then the loud voice of the sergeant again, telling us of the special bombs that had been dropped on Japan.

I have always been amazed at how one bit of news can change the entire atmosphere. It was like our life was beginning again. We began to talk about all kinds of things that we had put away, thinking that they would not happen. None of us slept very long that last night of our trip.

"We're going home! Alive!"

"We'll soon be going home!"

"They will discharge us now!"

Turns out that the discharge process was not such a simple matter. The Army had millions of men and women to discharge. They couldn't just tell them all, "Okay, you can go home now." It would be chaos. They had to give each service person a physical checkup, prepare their service records, financial clearing, etc. It was going to take time.

In the meantime, what did we do? We followed another old Army saying: "Hurry up and wait." We certainly knew enough of that experience, but this time we had one of the most popular beach resorts in California, Pismo Beach, right next-door. Pismo Beach is noted for surfing. I had never surfed before, but I was excited about trying, except we had no surfboards. One of our enterprising New York companions got the idea that if we took the covers off our army mattresses, filled them with air by running with them opened up, and then sealed them as best we could, we would have "surf-mattresses." What a sight that must have been, several hundred white-ballooned objects riding the surf and carrying men in GI undershorts. Some of our guys even stood up.

Three months later I finally got my discharge. They handed me my discharge papers and $300 travel money to find my way back to Maine. It was more money than I had ever had, but I was left to arrange my own journey home.

I took the bus to the railroad station in Los Angeles. Although I was alone, I never felt alone. There were thousands of military people getting discharged and all trying to get home. As I found my way into the station I was astounded at what I saw there. It looked like the entire United States military force laying on the floor, sitting on every seat and standing around. I asked someone what was going on. There were not enough trains to carry all of the discharged folk who wanted to go east. The trains were all delayed because of a railroad strike in Chicago.

I asked some of the guys there, "How long have you been waiting?"

"Three days."

They suggested I take a plane instead. The next morning, I took a taxi to the airport, stepped up to the window, gave them my name and said, "I'll take any plane going east." At 11:30 a.m. I heard a man call my name. "Mr. Marshall, we have a plane ready for you right now, going to El Paso, Texas."

"But I don't want to go to Texas. That's south. I want to go to Maine."

"You asked for a flight going east, and everything is east from California. Don't worry, when you get to Texas you will have no trouble getting a flight to Boston."

He was right! Four hours later I landed in El Paso and just a half hour later I was on a plane to Boston. I left Logan Airport and went to the train station for a ride to Portland. When I stepped up for my ticket I had just $25 left. It looked like I would have to hitchhike the last leg of my journey home. I decided to go into the USO canteen for a free cup of coffee and a donut. I got the idea of sending a telegram to my mother, who was the head volunteer of the USO in Portland to see if she could telegram me enough money to take the train home.

I think she would have even taken a taxi right from Portland to Boston to come and get me. She wired enough for the train ticket.

Three hours later I stepped off that train into Union Station in Portland, one of the happiest warriors to finally get back home alive, and for good this time! The war was over!!!

I suppose there are times in nearly every life when one must take a road that was not of one's own choosing. War was not a path I chose. I am glad I served in the infantry, because as a combat medic I was able to save lives instead of taking them.

The war was over. Those of us boys who had survived went home. We were not the same young boys who had left home three years ago. In many ways we were not boys any longer. We had aged in many ways and had seen the horrors of war. We would never be the same. Yet, we had also learned many things about the greater world. In time, I would set out again into the larger world to meet people who were very different from me. I didn't know it, but I was being prepared for another adventure far from Maine.

PART III: THE STORY OF MIZPAH

Meeting the Missionary

When I was a boy growing up in northern Maine, once a year a missionary came to visit us and tell of his or her experiences living and working with native people of faraway lands, especially Africa and India. I loved the idea of helping the people of those countries have a better life. The tales of that great missionary to Africa, David Livingston, especially intrigued me. I even dreamed of going to those places one day. Little did I know then, where those dreams might lead.

A Road Less Traveled

Several years after the war, when I was teaching in Vermont, I encountered the Reverend John De Boer, a man who grew up in India where his parents worked as missionaries. We met in a men's group at church. I was interested in the school he attended in India, the Katakana School for Children of missionaries and other American personnel. We talked about education, teaching, and church work. At the time my interest was purely academic, or at least I thought it was. I think John De Boer's wheels must have been turning, for shortly after our conversation, unbeknownst to me, he recommended us to the United Church Board of World Ministries for missionary work.

I was becoming fairly well established in the community of Vergennes, a small town in Vermont. I enjoyed my new job as assistant principal. Marvel, my wife, and I had bought a house. Our three kids, Paula, Alan, and Susan were all doing well in their schools and had friends. I would be foolish to leave. Why should I give up just about everything an American family could desire to teach somewhere else?

Still, travel and adventure were alluring to me. At the time I had been considering teaching in the Middle East, a region of the world that seemed exotic to me. I had just about made up my mind to accept a position at an American school in Lebanon when the letter from the Mission Board arrived.

The board sent us an application with many questions. We were confronted with the first of many difficult decisions. Were we earnestly sincere about this or were we just talking through our hats? Individually, Marvel and I were quite intrigued with the prospects of such a venture but we remained nonchalant about it for fear of influencing each other. I was fairly confident I could handle the educational part of the work, but felt quite inadequate carrying out the religious duties. With the casual attitude that there was nothing to lose by applying, we spent the better part of a week writing answers to questions such as: What personal attributes do you feel you have that would make you a success at overseas work? What place does Jesus Christ have in your life? What are your attitudes toward people of other races and nations?

Next Reverend Loy Long, the personnel secretary, came to our home in Vergennes and spent nearly a day with us and finally decided I may have the qualifications necessary for filling a position in Tarsus, Turkey, as the administrator of a high school. When I heard this, a strange feeling came over me. *Tarsus, Turkey, that was where Paul the Apostle came from! Now, I, Paul, am being called there?* Something was happening here. *Is this a call from God?* I wasn't even sure at that time that God did such things. But, it was "a road less traveled" and I am certainly drawn to those. The idea of travel seemed to create great excitement within us, the boat trip across the Atlantic, sighting the Rock of Gibraltar at the entrance of the Mediterranean Sea, perhaps a stopover in Rome, Genoa, or some other port in Italy, and finally sailing up the Bosporus to the beautiful city of Istanbul, trips to Palestine, Syria, Jerusalem, Egypt, Greece. All these dreams built up a beautiful romanticized vision of living and working in Turkey and the Middle East.

"Yes," I eagerly said, "I would be delighted to go to Turkey." We talked with professors and students who had lived and worked there. We studied the history of Turkey and the Turkish people. I started taking Turkish language classes. The Mission Board began to make plans for me and my family to take that momentous step in just four months.

We were scheduled to go by ship from New York City on a special Italian liner that would take us all the way to Istanbul. I could hardly wait.

In the meantime, we had to examine the real purpose behind the venture. We were asked to write autobiographies and submit an essay about our Christian beliefs. It is no simple task to put your own personal convictions into words. I, as many probably do, have a stereotyped idea of what a missionary should be: an extremely religious person, deeply committed to Christianity, well prepared to carry the word of the gospel and perhaps even die for it; one who had no doubts about his own convictions and felt a personal call to this work. I was not certain I met these requirements. Yet, I felt that if I was truthful in my statements, and if the Mission Board still wanted me, then I would go.

All forms completed, all statements of conviction prepared, autobiographies put into words, and the whole parcel delivered to Rev. Long. By the second week in January, we had nothing to do but sit back on the edges of our patience to await the decision of the board.

The last two weeks in January, I am convinced, are the two longest weeks in the year. On January 29th we received the following telegram, "Delighted to inform you that your appointment as missionaries is confirmed, but will consult further in field assignment. – Loy Long"

There were considerable mixed feelings in the Marshall family that night. We had been accepted to do a job, though we were not certain we could do it. We were overjoyed, but anxious about the last part of the telegram: "will consult further in field assignment." There seemed to be no question where we would be going. Turkey had become a common word in our home. All our thoughts had been directed to the Middle East, and the personnel secretary had recommended us for that position. What possibly could follow?

Then I got a call from the Mission Board, "Hello, Paul, this is the Pacific Area Secretary calling from the New York office. We know you have made your commitment to take the position in Turkey and we certainly want to assure you that we will not go against your wishes. However, we would like to construct a new high school in our mission field in Micronesia. We have been in contact with a builder, but what we desperately need at this venture is someone capable of developing an educational institution, someone who can also work to gain local support for the project. You have been highly recommended to us and we would like you to consider this position. We know that you have already committed yourself to the school in Turkey, but, at this time, the position in Micronesia is more important for the work of the mission. Please pray about it and give it your best thoughts, and let us know within thirty days of your decision."

Mike who? Micronesia? I had never heard of the place. They were asking us to go to this strange place and give five years of our lives to building and operating a school. They told us it was a small island called Moen, in a group of islands called The Eastern Caroline Islands. It sounded to me like the ends of the earth. Hastily, I ran to the world atlas, and after some deep searching I located the island group in the Pacific.

It would have been so easy to stick with our original plan of going to Turkey, but the board had asked us to consider this change and we felt that was the least we could do. For a month we searched our souls for the right answer. It is not easy to completely change your way of thinking once you have definitely made up you mind.

We searched for information about Micronesia, finding very little. We compared the opportunities in each location, specifically the educational opportunities. We would be gone for five years, and these would be formative years in the lives of our three teenage children. We considered the climate, travel, recreation, and opportunities for cultural growth. All of these seemed of the utmost importance. Our friends and acquaintances asked us important questions. *Why are you doing this? Is there good money in it? Why don't you stay at home, where there is plenty of good to be done right here in this country?*

Turkey had sounded a bit like my idea of heaven. Easy living, comfortable quarters, good schools for my children, exciting places to vacation and visit, a well-established school with well-trained teachers. All I had to do was take over a position that had been well established and operated. I would have to be insane to give all of that up. In Micronesia we would have no place to live, no place for our children to go to school. The hot, jungle would surely be a challenge for a Maine boy like myself. Turkey seemed to have more to offer us. We thought very little of how our talents could be put to the greatest use.

The days grew shorter. I began to think more and more about people of the world and their chances for a good life. I thought of Turkey, which, although they had their troubles, had been established for centuries. They had schools and universities. What about the people of Micronesia? I began desperately digging into all the material I could find about Micronesia. For centuries they had been under the domination of powerful world countries: Spain, the Netherlands, Germany, Japan, and now, Australia, Great Britain, France, and the United States. And what did they have to show for it: very few elementary schools, practically no government of their own, and no way to make a good living for themselves. I thought less and less about my needs, and instead asked, *where is the greatest need for me? What have I to give to them?* It scared me. I did not feel qualified to build or start a school. I had never set up an entire curriculum for a high school.

Thoughts seemed to be haunting me, *what if I don't go to Micronesia? Suppose the Mission Board cannot get anyone to go? What about all of those kids in Micronesia? How will they get an education that will fit them for a rapidly advancing world? Do we want other countries to take control over their lives again? How can they be brought into the 21st century with a good educational background, as well as a solid Christian basis for living a fruitful life?* A thought began to enter my mind, *what would God want me to do?*

Thirty days after the phone call from the Mission Board I sat at my desk at the end of the school day. It was quiet, and I began to cry. I had never cried like that before. I just let it all go out. And then, I stopped. It was if a heavy load had been lifted off my shoulders. I felt good, real good. The words of Robert Frost's poem came to me, "I took the road less traveled, and it has made all the difference." I knew where I was going. I made the call.

The Journey

We had planned to travel to Micronesia during the summer of 1964. There was no set timeline. We were simply waiting for word from the mission that a temporary home had been built for us in Micronesia. The Mission Board had taken on Ted Lewis, a builder from St. Louis, Missouri. He was a fine man, and very capable, but he had his own ideas about how to start building a school in Micronesia. Instead of going straight to Micronesia to start building, he started a tour of the Orient to find the best places to buy materials for the construction, and to figure out how to get them to the island, and taking his time about it too. He also took his family with him and was having a wonderful time. I can't blame him for that.

In the meantime we put our house on the market, moved into our little camp on Little Sebago Lake in Maine, and just waited. Marvel started homeschooling the kids. It was September. Then October. I finally got really disturbed told the Mission Board, "We are going now, or I'm not going, because I can't wait any longer. It's been three months."

They said, "Well, we don't know how you're going to get out there or where you'll live. We don't think your living quarters will be ready."

I said, "Well, I'll find out myself."

Since there was no hurry to get there I thought, let's make a trip of it. I wanted to take my kids across the country by train. We took the bus to Boston and picked up the train. We stopped first in Chicago, and went to the Natural Museum of Art. Then we got on this lovely train called the Rock Island Rocket. It was the most beautiful passenger train I've ever seen. But it was a long trip. We finally got into San Francisco. There was no hurry to get to our final destination, so we spent a week walking the old Spanish streets, going to the Spanish churches, and down to Fisherman's Wharf and Alcatraz. It was just wonderful. It was part of my kid's education. I felt it was good for them.

I told the Mission Board that I didn't want to go on a fancy cruise ship. I wanted to go in a cargo ship, like the early missionaries

did. I wanted us to con-
nect with that history.
The board made all the
arrangements for the
trip, but no one men-
tioned that our ship was
loaded with ammuni-
tion for Vietnam.

The ship was called
the USS President
McKinley. Our journey
would take us to the
island of Guam in the
Mariana Islands. From
there, we would either go
by inter-island cargo ship
or plane to Truk, our destination. We were the
only passengers except for
a sailor's wife who was
going out to Guam to
meet her husband. We
had our own steward,
and he made sure there
was fruit in our room
every morning. We had

Marm and Dad wave goodbye at South Station,
Boston, October, 1964

Daughters Paula and Susan in the dining car on the
Rock Island Rocket going west, November 1964

three cabins: my son had one, my two daughters had the other, and my
wife and I had the third. We ate with the captain in the dining room
and had wonderful meals. Oh, the food was fantastic. There was nothing
to do except walk the deck. I remember, 33 times around the deck was
a mile, because I used to walk it a lot. There were flying fish flying over
us all the time, and we'd see whales way off. You could see thunderstorms
flashing off in the distance and the rest of the sky would be blue. The
sea was absolutely beautiful, just beautiful. The trip lasted 14 days.

We didn't know what to expect for the next leg of the trip. We had no idea how long it would take to get from Guam to Truk, where we were headed. We didn't know if there would be anyone there to meet us. We had no names of people to look for when we did arrive. We had no place to stay. The mission superintendent, Harold Hamilin, was on the islands of Pohnpei, and he knew we were coming, but didn't know when. He was, of course, another 500 miles away from Truk. But I was not afraid.

Ever since we left Maine the children asked me so many questions and most of them I could not answer. Yet, they still took a can-do attitude to all of the difficulties we confronted. All during our trip I taught them songs I sang as a child. Whenever I thought they were a bit concerned I would sing a song and they would join in. It seemed to work most of the time.

Our only stop on our ocean trip was to be the island of Guam in the Mariana Islands. After 14 days at sea, we pulled into Guam it was about five o'clock at night, and the dock was empty. There was nobody there. They put a gangplank down and we walked off the boat. It felt real funny because I had no idea what to do, where to go.

An Army pick-up truck showed up and a young man got out and said, "Marshall?"

I said, "Yeah."

He said, "The Baptist Mission heard you were coming and they sent me to get you."

I'll never forget his name, Norman Wether. He took us to Agana where he had established a mission out of Quonset huts the Navy left behind after World War II. He'd made some of the huts into a little inn, and that's where we stayed that night.

Norman also filled us in on the ship and plane schedule. A ship would sail to each island, leaving once a month. Much to my disappointment, the ship had left the day before, so my dream of reaching Truk by boat was not a possibility. There was a plane that flew into Truk once a week, and we had just missed that too. We would have to spend a week in Guam. After one night at Norman's "inn" we moved to the Micronesian Hotel, a place set up for native Micronesian government officials to stay in as they moved back and forth from island to island. After talking to some people I met there, I decided to use the week to visit Saipan, where the Trust Territory Headquarters were. Because the high school was not going to be a government school, it was necessary to obtain a charter.

The next day, I caught a plane to Saipan, the capital of the Mariana Islands. When I arrived I could see the airport was way out in the countryside, jungle all around. I inquired about a taxi, and they said, "There aren't any taxis here. The only cars are government cars, and they're all gone."

I said, 'Well, how am I going to get to the Trust Territory headquarters?" which was about five miles around the island.

One of the natives came up and said, "I know a woman, Rosie, who has a car. She will rent it."

I said, "Where?"

"Well, it's down the road about two miles."

"How am I going to get there?"

Well, there happened to be a car at the airport and they took me to Rosie's. So we went out and found Rosie, who owned a little store. Sure enough she had a little old Beetle and she wanted $5 a day for it, which was a small fortune in 1963 in Micronesia.

I rented the car and drove five miles down a dirt road through native villages to Capitol Hill. It was a beautiful place, built by the U.S. Navy, wonderful homes and facilities. I met with the Commissioner of Education, who sat down and quickly issued me a charter permit.

I thanked him, and said, "Well, I've got to get going to catch a flight back to Guam."

He said, "Well, the plane doesn't go until next week."

So I was stuck on Saipan for the week. A week later I finally got back to my family waiting for me in Guam and we caught the plane the very next day to Truk.

Paul on USS President McKinley, Nov. 1964

The Marshalls arrive on Moen Island, Truk. Paul with a new friend, a Filipino cameraman, at the airport, November 1963

As we approached the islands of Truk, we could see out of the window the Island of Moen complete with its surrounding reef islands, which was to be our home for the next four years. It was truly exciting to see where we would be spending those coming years in such a beautiful and unique place. We had traveled over 8,000 miles by train, boat, and plane to reach our final destination.

The flight attendant suggested we look out our window to see the landing strip, our final stop. Our eyes grew wide. Someone asked, "Are we really going to land on that little short piece of runway?" The answer to the question came swiftly. We saw a very short strip of concrete with ocean water on both ends. I imagine even a child's paper plane would have difficulty landing there, let alone a big 60-passenger airplane. I think we all held our breath as our plane touched its wheels on solid ground at the very rim of the landing field. That was fine, but would it be able to stop before it went off over the other end? It did stop, exactly at the edge of the other end, with very little land to spare.

The next concern was: Where do we go from here? We had no plan, no guide. As I reflect back, I am convinced God knew all of my inadequacies, because whenever I met up with seemingly impossible situations help always seemed to come from somewhere.

I stepped down the stairs from the plane and saw many people milling about, but no welcoming committee. The airport terminal consisted of several thatched-roof structures that looked as if a good wind might turn them over. Strips of rusty corrugated metal sheets held them together. As we lugged our suitcases towards the largest of these structures a man approached us.

"Are you Paul Marshall?"

"Yeah."

"Tuck Wah Lee," he says. "I am a missionary too. I heard you were coming, but I had no idea when. I've been meeting the plane every week."

At last we found someone who actually knew something. We could finally breathe a sigh of relief at the end of our long journey. Though it had been exhausting and confusing, I had not been afraid. I've been that way most of my life. As a kid getting lost in the woods, I never felt like I was lost. I knew we would find our way.

An Island Tour

Tuck Wah Lee became our guide to Truk. He was a Japanese-Hawaiian ordained minister with the Congregational Church of America. For several years he served in various mission stations in Micronesia and was presently the superintendent of the local churches in Truk. He could speak Trukese and Ponapean languages and was a great help to me in both of those districts.

At the airport we all climbed into a pickup truck Tuck Wah Lee had borrowed from the American Compound. He drove us down through the village and told us he had arranged a temporary home for us, news which eased our worried hearts. We came to a stop at what looked like a group of abandoned structures from WWII. He showed

Typical island travel

us our new home, a Quonset hut, long ago abandoned by the U.S. Navy, which had been in control of the Micronesian Islands after the defeat of the Japanese in WWII. Our hut was special because it had been the Bachelor Officer Quarters, the BOQ. It was still in fairly good condition and it looked as though it would suffice as a temporary home until our permanent quarters at the new school could be completed.

It was dark by the time we arrived, but we were amazed to find a few lights on around the area; even our abandoned hut had electricity. Tuck Wah wished us good night and said not to worry about anything because he would be back in the morning.

I looked around at our sparse accommodations, no appliances, no furniture, just a few used mattresses Tuck Wah had found for us. I thought back to some of my conversations with the Mission Board. They had expressed concern about where we would live until the school was built. I had told them, "We are a hiking and camping family and can handle roughing it. We might even enjoy it." At that time I had no idea just how long we would have to "rough it."

In the morning we awoke to a new and exciting world. Our hut faced the lagoon, and we could see other islands far off in the distance.

Behind the hut we saw a very high green mountain. We later discovered it was covered with massive breadfruit trees, which provided a popular local food. The kids could hardly wait to get out and start running, and I didn't blame them, but Marvel and I feared they might wander too far and get lost. We had no idea how the locals would react to them.

My thoughts were focused on: What's next? How do we get food? How do we get water? How do we make a home from almost nothing? I had no answers, but Tuck Wah Lee did. I hoped he would soon show up again, which, within an hour, he did.

Weekly food preparation in Truk consisted of the gathering and cooking of breadfruit.

Tuck Wah came in his pickup with an electric stove, a refrigerator, and two helpers. The appliances looked rusty and used, but as soon as we connected them to an outlet both began working. We had one more great surprise. We had not expected to have running water, especially a toilet still in action. As usual, Tuck Wah had the answer. "Lo and behold," right behind the BOQ, a building with toilets and showers.

Though the showers were inoperable, the toilets still worked.

Happy to help, Tuck Wah offered to give us a tour of the island. I was especially eager to see the building site for our new school. We hopped in the truck and headed down to the site. I had not given much thought to the sort of infrastructure I would find on Truk. I suppose I should not have been surprised when the pavement ended and we started bumping along on an unattended gravel road. There were no drainage ditches and huge water puddles pooled alongside the road after a rain from two days before. Our ride took us right along the shoreline and we could see out across the lagoon.

We noticed several modern-looking residences, which seemed out of place in Truk. Tuck Wah, our trusty informant, told us they had originally housed the most important Japanese officers. On the other side of the road, it was a different story. We began to see the homes of the native people, the real people of Truk. Their homes were built with thatched roofs, rusty sheets of metal on the sides of some of them and half-walls constructed of bamboo branches and banana leaves or palms. The houses were grouped in twos; we later learned one served as a sleeping place and the other was the daily living quarters. They cooked all of their meals outside on a bed of coral rock using dried coconut shells for fuel. We had to be careful not to run over the pigs that kept dashing in front of the truck, or the hens and chickens fluttering about in our path.

Continuing along the shore road, we saw concrete structures in the water just a short distance from the shore, partially covered with water. There were several openings just above the water line in each structure. Again, our wise leader informed us that these were known as *bunkers*, Japanese structures with guns.

This tour introduced us to two very different worlds. The first world belonged to a simple village way of life, living day to day, merely keeping alive, and perhaps even enjoying some of it. The second world was the one we had just come from, a world often filled with ugliness, hate, power, and a lack of consideration for the simple lives of people such as the Trukese. Over-powering countries had ruled Micronesia for many centuries and treated the people poorly. I wanted them to realize it does not have to be that way, to know there is a source of love to help them to have more valuable lives. I saw this as part of my mission.

Out in the water we saw towers of rusty ships and the remains of an airplane, its nose buried in the depths of the water, but its wings and tail revealed it was the wreckage of an American fighter plane's last flight.

As we passed by the Trukese homes, we saw women dressed only in skirts. They would be outside the home doing a magnificent job of sweeping the ground with homemade brooms made of palm branches. When the women saw us coming they hurriedly pulled up their skirts to cover their breasts as we passed by. As soon we were out of sight the skirts were pulled back down. This happened at nearly every home we passed. Tuck Wah explained: the early missionaries taught the women that exposing their sexual parts to the opposite sex was sinful. The Trukese women knew American men were excited by the sight of a woman's breast, while the Trukese men were excited by a woman's legs. When a woman pulls her skirt up to cover her breasts her legs are revealed, so she has to move quickly to cover the right parts in the presence of either American or Trukese men.

Continuing on our way we saw a church, a beautifully-constructed stone and concrete building, steeple and all, with a wonderful view out over the lagoon. All around it was an immense dense jungle. Tuck Wah, said, "We are at looking at the school site!"

I had expected an area with some vegetation, but this was all jungle, 21 acres of it, and much of it sloping up toward a beautiful mountain peak. All I could think was what a task it would be to clear enough land to build the school buildings we had planned. Yet, I could hardly wait to start. The property was flat near the church but most of it sloped upward, and upward toward the mountain. *How can I build a school and several buildings on this seemingly impossible piece of land?* We had no bulldozer. My only hope was that the contractor had been wise enough to prepare for the conditions.

Very near to the church stood a small aluminum building. Tuck Wah told us that was his home. We stopped and entered the house where we met Tuck Wah's wife, Alice. What a pleasure! Alice was also of Japanese-Hawaiian descent, and we soon saw she was a perfect match for Tuck Wah. Between the two of them, I knew our stay in Truk would work out beautifully.

In those first couple of days we settled into our Quonset hut. We made our first venture to the compound store, a modern grocery store that served the families living in the American compound, which was only a half-mile from our hut. It wasn't so different from stores back home, though the prices seemed considerably higher. Inside the compound was also an excellent movie theater, paved roads, and even an auto repair garage, something very few Trukese needed. The other Americans' homes looked as nice and modern as houses back in the States, and perhaps even better. Looking around the compound you might think you were in a quiet residential area in the United States.

I also found the Truk District Offices inside the compound and introduced myself to Alan Macquarrie, the district administrator, who was highly in favor of our plans to build a school. I was pleased. We certainly would need all of the support we could get.

Our children, Paula, Susan, and Alan made an active playground in the front plaza of our hut, and many of the native children also discovered it was a safe and exciting place to play. Our children quickly made friends and adapted to the new culture of the island.

We soon discovered we did not need blankets or quilts, because it was too hot to cover up at night. Though we did need something to keep the geckos from cuddling up too close to us. It was fascinating to watch small lizards shed their tails and produce new ones. The geckos were a bit of a nuisance, but not nearly as troublesome as the huge island rats. Long ago whaleboats and other ships stopped on the islands of Micronesia and rats scurried off the ships and made themselves very much at home. There was always plenty of food year round, especially the coconuts that often covered the ground, and the rats flourished. We awoke one night to a strange sound. After turning on a light we saw three huge rats atop our refrigerator. This same event continued for a few nights until we were able to get some good-sized traps, which discouraged our night visitors, and finally allowed us to have a full night's sleep.

Tuck Wah went back to his work with the island churches and pastors spread out over the entire lagoon. When he left us on our own, I felt a bit unsettled, but I was also anxious to get things rolling. Marvel was busy with the children's correspondence courses and making plans for her contributions to the future school. The children were as excited as ever about everything, so they certainly were not bored. I decided I could leave them on their own for the day. I had no vehicle, but early in the morning of the third day I started walking the more than two miles to the school site.

A School Called Mizpah

During those first few days I began to realize how poorly prepared everything was. I had expected to have housing ready for my family. I had expected the construction of the school would be well on its way. I expected my coming to Micronesia to be broadcast all over the Trust Territory by our field superintendent. Nothing was ready. I don't lay all of the blame on the Mission Board. I should have made certain these matters were covered.

I felt I was walking into uncharted territory with many responsibilities and no map of how to find my way. I had been asked to build a school called Mizpah High School of Micronesia. The name came from Charles Heuser, a missionary who had served in the Truk District before my term. He had dreamed of a high school for the Micronesians. After he returned from his mission work in Micronesia he went on to serve the Mizpah United Church of Christ in Hopkins, Minnesota. He named his dream Mizpah High School after the church he had come to love. It was an appropriate name, he felt, as the word in Hebrew means "watchtower" or a "lookout," and symbolized an agreement between men with God as their witness.

My new friends, the Trukese wamperons

The word *Mizpah* can be interpreted in different ways. You find it in the Book of Genesis in the story of Jacob and his Uncle Laban. Jacob made a contract with his uncle that he would work seven years for Laban, so that he might marry Laban's daughter, Rachel, which was not an unusual agreement in that time and culture. But Laban had taken back his word and cheated Jacob. This occurred again and finally after 20 years, Jacob escaped from his uncle taking with him a considerable number of sheep as well as two of Laban's daughters, Leah and Rachel, who had become Jacob's wives.

Laban chased after Jacob as he fled to his homeland. Laban caught up with Jacob at a selected place and they set up a heap of stones to permanently mark the place. There they made a covenant, which sounded as though it might be a friendly deal, but could be read more like a warning not to ever meet again or there might be a different situation. "May the Lord watch between me and thee while we are absent from one another." There are many interpretations to this story. It could be taken as a threat, or as a well-meant goodbye and that God would take care of them both while they were separated. The statement has become, to most Christians, a "fare-thee-well" statement known as the Mizpah Benediction. "May God bless you and keep you," is often used as a parting blessing in church ceremonies. The name *Mizpah* is given to places and villages, and I believe Heuser intended it as a "watchtower" for the people of Micronesia.

Along with Heuser and the Mission Board I wanted Mizpah to serve as a beacon for the people of Micronesia. Even after my brief introduction to the island, I could see the need for such a school, and somehow we would have to build it. Yet, there was so much that needed to happen before the school that existed only in our minds could become a watchtower to Micronesia. The idea was simply daunting. All I could see at this point was a jungle. How would I turn it into Mizpah, a modern school comparable with top-quality American education?

Finding myself at this unexpected point, I sat down and made a practical plan of things I could immediately begin work on.

1. Get better acquainted with all of the people I will be working with and those I might need to call upon for help: the people of the local villages, the island chiefs, and pastors of local churches.
2. Contact all of the mission stations within the jurisdiction of the Mission Board.
3. Do whatever I can do to get the construction of the school underway until the arrival of the contractor.
4. Start planning the school curriculum, school schedule. Order the necessary student books, as well as the needs of the teachers.

There was really so much more, and I could go on listing all that had to be done before we would become a fully-operating organization. I was perhaps more than slightly overwhelmed by what I saw facing me. *Could I accomplish everything necessary to get the school going in the short time that I had to serve?* I thought of the school I left in Vermont with its school board, superintendent, and a complete staff of teachers. I felt somewhat inadequate to the task. I had to serve all of these roles.

Marm and Dad taught me early on, "Do your best for what you have to do today. Then tomorrow's work will be much easier." What could I start working on right away? I've always thought, if you have to do a certain task that involves other people, then the first thing to do is to become friendly with those you have to share your work with. I needed to make some friends. Soon I'd need help recruiting workers for the construction and later help recruiting students.

The Mission Board hoped the local people would provide most of the labor to build the school. Certainly importing outside labor would be extremely costly. Yet the local people were not skilled at modern construction. I saw my first goal, to get acquainted with the village pastors around the lagoon. As respected leaders in their communities they could encourage their parishioners to help us.

Again, I turned to Tuck Wah for help. He was well acquainted with all the pastors, who, in turn, held him in great respect. As it turns out Tuck Wah already had a plan in mind and was eager to put it into operation, though he did not share his plan with me at the time.

Two days later, in the early afternoon, Trukese men began to arrive and sit on the patio in front of the BOQ. I saw about 20 men gathered and I began to wonder what was going on. I had been told the local people were not allowed on the grounds unless they worked for one of the Americans. Then I saw Tuck Wah himself enter the plaza, followed by his wife Alice and several women carrying baskets. The men all stood and greeted Tuck Wah and the women. The whole scene came to life. The baskets the women carried contained food, bunches of bananas, beautiful leis, and head decorations. We knew we were a part of something important. Everyone stepped forward and each greeted us. These men were all *wamperons* (the Trukese name for pastor) and the women were their wives. By the end of the afternoon we knew we had lots and lots of friends in Truk.

I had accomplished, with a lot of Tuck Wah's help, my goal of making friends. The first step had been taken. With the wamperons as friends at my side we were on our way to building our watchtower for Micronesia, our Mizpah.

Typhoon

Our first few days in Truk were quite beautiful, bright sun every day, and the moon lighting the lagoon each evening. It appeared as though we were going to enjoy the weather of Truk, at least for a while. We had been told typhoons sometimes attacked these islands, but we had no warning of how often they appeared or how dangerous they were.

Just a couple of days after our welcoming party it began to rain and wind began blowing from all directions. Then Tuck Wah showed up early in the morning with a warning that a typhoon was predicted and would be hitting Truk in one or two days. He told us it would not be safe to remain at the BOQ because the building was old and could not withstand heavy winds. Only the American buildings on the island had special typhoon-protection areas. The local folk would go to the caves located partway up the mountainside just behind us for protection and Tuck Wah said we should join them.

That was our first introduction to the caves. There were many of them, he told us, located all around the lagoon. Most were not natural caves, but had been burrowed out of the mountainside during World War II by the Japanese as gun bases.

Tuck Wah told us one of the wamperons would be coming very soon to lead us to one of the caves. His final word was that we should prepare enough food for at least three days in the caves. Tuck Wah then left us.

Fortunately we were within walking distance of the grocery store, so off we went to find food to sustain us for three days. We returned with sandwich fixings, some sweets, and cans of drinks. We packed the food into small backpacks, and very soon Wamperon Andon, whom we met recently at the welcoming party, arrived at our hut, telling us that he would take us to the cave as soon as we were ready. "Are you ready?"

I wish I could convey the feelings I had about what was happening and where we were going. It wasn't fear, as I think I felt that we were in good hands, but there was a sense of "lost-ness" about what was happening to us. We had just begun to feel that everything was going quite well and now there was a possibility we would lose everything. I didn't reveal my feelings to my wife and children. I tried to treat the situation as if it were a special "exploring trip." Actually, I recall that they seemed to be having a good time.

We started off along the shore road following Andon. Looking back, I noticed quite a number of local folk following just a short distance behind us. They were all carrying baskets loaded with food. We had not yet learned what the Trukese diet consisted of, but we would very soon meet up with that knowledge.

Continuing along the abandoned road as it went up and up into the mountain we could occasionally catch glimpses of some of the caves. At one spot I remember even seeing a huge gun peering out over the edge.

The local folk were still following us, but kept a fairly good distance behind us. It seemed the whole village was walking behind us. I wondered how many of us would have to share a cave. Andon assured me there were several caves and plenty of room for all. Andon's English was very good; he had received training in a special school for pastors and teachers.

The going was still fairly easy and about an hour later we came in sight of a cave with a large gun sticking out of it. Andon began talking loud enough for all to hear him (preachers are trained to do that). I did not know what he was saying, but soon some of the Trukese began moving into the nearest cave. The rest of them began moving ahead. I could not see what lay ahead as the path began to curve around the mountain wall, but there must have been several more caves in that direction. I am sure this was not the first time the Trukese had gone through this experience.

Then Andon led us into the first cave, right past the cave with the big gun. I had imagined there would be space only for the gun, but upon entering, I saw there was considerable space behind it. I had not counted the number of people who had gone into the cave before us but it looked as though we might be in a somewhat crowded space.

It was such a help to have Andon leading us. We could not have done it without him. The local folk seemed to have a great deal of respect for him also, and his skill with English certainly helped us to feel quite comfortable.

Don't get the idea that this cave was the Waldorf-Astoria type. Our Trukese friends were either sitting or lying against the cave walls, but I noticed a somewhat spacious area off to the side, which Andon softly indicated would be ours. I wondered where we were to go to relieve ourselves. Andon advised us to go out of the cave for such situations.

We felt a bit unsettled that first night. There was hardly space enough for all five of us to lay down along with our packs, but it reminded us of the times we had shared a lean-to while hiking in the Green Mountains of Vermont. I have always been astounded how human beings can adapt to seemingly impossible situations when called upon to do so.

The wind came up strong during the night and rain was being blown into the entrance of the cave, yet we were dry and felt well protected. Sleeping was difficult and I began telling stories to the children, which soon put them to sleep. I hardly slept at all, and that was partially because the Trukese folk, who were very close to us, continued to talk well into the night. Of course there was no lighting system in our "accommodations," which made it quite difficult to move around after dark. It was difficult to avoid stepping on our neighbors.

Morning came with more wind and heavy rains. We were enclosed there for two and a half days. Looking back I am amazed at how well we handled those difficult situations. I have become certain it is how we handle the difficult situations we meet up with in life that strengthen us rather than weaken us. Marvel and I tried our best to keep the children from fear and boredom, and they were wonderful. Often in their later lives they have expressed how much their Micronesian experience strengthened them.

In just those two and a half days we got to know the Trukese folk in several ways: what they eat for daily food, how they cook their meals, their ways of expressing happiness, their respect for those who try to lead them. Occasionally they would sing hymns along with Andon. The Trukese hymns are the same as our American ones, except for the language, because the early missionaries taught them to them. So it was fun to sing along. The Trukese have wonderful voices and can very easily come up with their own harmonizing.

Our picnic type food was okay and the Trukese kept bringing us some of their food, which we found a bit difficult to eat, but also difficult to refuse. Mostly it consisted of pre-cooked taro, a starchy plant root, not un-like potato, along with some pre-cooked fish, with the heads still attached! I lost my taste for fish. We also shared our sandwiches with them and they were excited about that.

We began to feel quite comfortable with our neighbors, after singing with them and sharing food and listening to their singing and constant chatter. Andon told us much about the people. The whole experience helped us to feel our future was going to be pleasant, rewarding, and even enjoyable.

Awakening early on our third day, it sounded like the rain had eased up, and although there was still some wind swishing around, Andon decided it was safe enough for us to make our downward trek. What a joyous time. The Trukese were again singing. Our packs were light. It was still raining some, but there was practically no wind. We were safe and sound.

As we walked down the mountain Andon told us more about his people and the island. It was such wonderful way to get to know them and their history and the difficult life they had suffered under the Japanese, as well as the previous occupations by the Spanish and the Germans. He also told us most people could expect to find their thatched roof houses destroyed by the typhoon when they returned to their village. Fortunately since they owned no furniture and very few personal possessions they would suffer little loss. In perhaps a strange way, I have thought that the incidence of the typhoon was a lesson to help us to have a deeper understanding of the life of the Trukese.

Returning to the BOQ we found our hut was okay, except for a couple of window blinds tangled beyond repair. It was nothing compared to the damage done to most of the thatched huts of our new friends in Mwan Village.

I was anxious to begin my work at the school site, but was not too eager to see what damage might have been done there. I began my walk down through the village, and it was truly a mess. The road maintenance crews from the district compound were hard at work trying to get the road cleared of the many palm trees lying across it. As I approached the village I could understand why they had to find a safe place to ride out the storm. There was hardly a recognizable structure. I wished I could help them, but I had my own problems and had no idea how to make new thatch.

I continued my walk through the village until I came upon the school site. The church appeared to be okay; it was constructed of 12-inch thick concrete walls with no glass in the windows, so nothing appeared to be damaged. Tuck Wah's aluminum house also stood solid with no apparent damage. As I approached the school site it looked quite different than when I had first seen it. There were palm trees all bent over, and the banana plants had lost most of their fruit. It looked like they were bent over and weeping at the loss. The sight of the damaged jungle did not bother me so much as my next task, which was to get my first crew of Trukese men to come and start clearing the site.

Living In Two Worlds

Trukese children

I felt I was living in two worlds: the American world and the Micronesian world. The Americans living on Truk lived a life that was not so different from life in America. They had electricity, running water, air conditioning, automobiles, movie theaters, a hotel with a barroom, a hospital, a supermarket with all the same foods you could buy in stores back in America.

The Trukese world had barely changed for hundreds of years. They lived just as their ancestors had lived. The biggest change was religion. Even though outsiders had imposed new religious ideas there for centuries, they had not entirely wiped out earlier beliefs.

My family and I found ourselves living on the edge of both worlds, and we quite enjoyed it. Our children found it very interesting to play with the island children and learn their ways, as well as teaching the island children our ways.

I enjoyed my daily walks down through Mwan Village. Every now and then someone, always a man, would step up to me, and after bowing slightly would offer me a coconut-cocktail, which was a complete coconut with its knob cut off, opening up to the milky liquid inside the nut. Delicious.

I have been asked how I felt about the Trukese bowing to me. They did not actually bend at the waist, but rather they gave a slow nod of the head, accompanied by laying a hand on the opposite arm. I always felt it signified a show of respect more than anything else. I even tried it in the presence of a Trukese person whom I respected highly, such as Chief Petrus, and I was never corrected by anyone.

Paul wearing an ancient Trukese fighting outfit, in front of the BOQ, Nov. 1963

We also started to notice an absence of watches and clocks; the Trukese had a different attitude about time. We wanted to attend the local church so I asked one of the church attendants what time the service began.

"When the wamperon gets here."

That certainly made a lot of sense to me.

Church was a great place to observe the two cultures at work. We expected the local island churches to be patterned after the Protestant New England style since all of the island churches in our mission were begun by early New England missionaries. Upon entering the Logan Memorial Church, we expected to be met by ushers, but there was no one at the entrance. There were no pews or any kind of seating; everyone was sitting or squatting on the floor, women on the left, and men on the right. We immediately took our proper places on the floor. At first it felt a bit strange to separate our family as we had always customarily sat together during church services. We wanted to be accepted by the local folk and made up our minds to become a part of the island culture as much as we could, rather than to impose our culture on them.

The church had five gothic-style glassless window openings located fairly close to the ground. The sight of several men standing by windows

Logan Memorial and Mizpah boat landing

caught my eye when I first entered the sanctuary. They were very quiet and still and remained there during the entire service. Tuck Wah later explained that those men smoked cigarettes, an action considered a sin by the Trukese, and thus they were not allowed into the sanctuary.

The wamperon conducted the entire service in Trukese. Singing in church was an interesting experience. There were no hymnbooks. One person stood up and in a loud voice struck a note. Immediately the congregation stood and sang. Surprisingly, we found the hymns familiar to us and we could sing our own English words. The local folk looked at us with surprise and big smiles on their faces. Of course their songs were familiar to us. All of the early missionaries had stemmed from New England Congregational churches. We soon learned not to be so surprised by this, and I could see that attending the local churches was going to be a great joy.

The Work Crew

I had a rough map of the mission property. I could see there was a lot of work to be done. The mission expected me to begin classes in September. That was less than a year away and all I had were blueprints and a jungle. I began by working out where the property lines were. This proved to be a rather difficult task, made harder by the coconut tree laws. As a native you can plant a coconut tree wherever you want, and that tree is yours. No matter if it's on your property or not. So while mapping the property line, I had to keep in my mind the tree on this side belongs to so and so, the tree on that side belongs to someone else. I had worked in forestry so I knew how to survey, and I started laying out some ground, but we couldn't do anything because I had no idea how we were going to get this jungle down. I needed help.

Tuck Wah and the wamperons came up with a plan to bring volunteer workers to the site. The workers would find their own places to sleep and eat meals. We would supply a noon meal at the site. These men were all volunteers. Their work was seen as a gift to the mission, because they wanted their children to attend the school.

Each week Tuck Wah and I gathered up a different crew of volunteers from the seven island villages in the lagoon. We picked them up on Monday mornings and returned them on Saturdays. This way no one would be gone very long from their village or have to miss church on Sundays.

Tuck Wah had an outboard boat that could carry, at most, only eight men, and even that number would settle the boat quite low in the water. Most of the time the lagoon waters were calm and unaffected by the swells of the outer ocean. We could make the trip in less than two hours. Tuck Wah wanted me to go on each trip because he wanted my company. He also felt the men would have greater respect for me, and it would pep up their enthusiasm.

Saturday arrived and Tuck Wah and I headed across the lagoon to the first village. I noticed Tuck Wah was an excellent boatman. (He had worked on a fishing boat in his hometown of Hilo in Hawaii.)

Nuyeh ("Happy New Year") in the makeshift cooking shack at the construction site

The Truk Lagoon is a circular lagoon with a diameter of 40 miles and the villages are scattered over most of the high islands.

I could hardly wait for the first crew. I was anxious to begin working with the men, but I also realized it might be somewhat difficult since I could not speak their language.

Our first pick-up was full of anticipation and excitement. The men jabbered all the way to Mwan village. Tuck Wah was quite fluent in the language and occasionally joined in the conversation. Tuck Wah explained to the group what we had to do and how it would be done. He tried to make it clear that I would be in charge. I worried how I would be able to direct the work when Tuck Wah was not there to interpret for me.

We arrived near noontime and Tuck Wah's wife Alice prepared a big pot of rice, fish, and taro for the volunteer workers. While we sat on the ground beside the church eating our lunch some of the village folk wandered by and started talking with the men.

An older man with a great big smile came forward and talked with Tuck Wah for several minutes. He spoke in English, clear enough so I was able to understand him, although his usage was somewhat mixed.

Except for some of the wamperons, he was the first local person I had heard speaking English. I approached and Tuck Wah introduced him, saying: "This is Nuyeh." It sounded very much like "New Year." Wearing his big smile he spoke, "Me, Happy New Year," pointing at himself.

Later, Tuck Wah told me Nuyeh had worked as a groundskeeper for some Americans while the U.S. Navy was stationed in Truk, and he learned a fair amount of English on the job. When the Americans heard his name and saw the natural smile always on his face they nicknamed him "Happy New Year." Strangely enough, my first meeting with Happy New Year was close to the start of a new year, 1964.

Nuyeh was an elder and held positions in the local church, and so the Trukese respected him and always called him by his given name. (The village folk generally respected the elderly because they believed old people hold the secrets of life and might have special powers over life itself, and, if they were disturbed by something you did, they could use those powers against you.) Nuyeh became my right hand and a great friend.

Tuck Wah and I took a vast number of trips over a period of nearly six months. One trip in particular still remains very clear in my memory. One day we came into a bay to pick up our next crew. There was no dock to tie up to. (Many of the villages had no need to dock boats larger than a canoe. People simply carried their boat home.)

There was no one waiting on shore. "Where are they?" Thinking they might be in another bay, Tuck Wah backed the boat around to leave when the boat hit a coral shoal. I got out of the boat to help get us off the rocks.

Tuck Wah shouted, "Stop!" I did.

Then I saw the reason for alarm. Less than 20 feet from our boat, there were at least three or four sharks moving in our direction. I got back into the boat, and the sharks came uncomfortably close. We were safe in the boat, even though it was slanting and had begun to fill in with water. Somehow the sharks became discouraged and went off on their way outward. Then we freed our boat from the rocks just as our six-man crew came into sight. I was beginning to accept the fact that the Trukese were not as concerned with time as Americans. Our trips

became more comfortable and I truly relished the visits to the villages
with Tuck Wah.

Work at the site was finally underway. Nuyeh had been on the job
for only two days and had things moving along as though he had always
been there. He quickly constructed a cooking shack, island style, with
a thatched roof built over a rough stone fireplace. Somehow he got
hold of a huge metal kettle just the right size for cooking rice for a big
group of hungry men. He also found some discarded metal rods the
Japanese had used to grill fish. I will never forget his pleasant smile and
quiet but firm way of getting the men to do as he and I wished.

I planned for our work at the site to begin at eight o'clock in the
morning on Mondays. We would work until noon each day, eat a meal
of rice and fish, and then work through the afternoon until five o'clock.
We often took an hour break in the heat of the afternoon so the men
could run to the shore and jump in. It was December and on Truk the
average temperature seldom went below 85 degrees Fahrenheit, while
back home in New England the average temperature hardly went above
32 degrees. It took considerable time for our family to become acclimated to the difference.

The clearing of the site was going very well. The men always seemed
to enjoy whatever they were doing. I never had to push them in their
work, and they were always on time every morning. I am sure Nuyeh
had something to do with that. They were a pleasure to work with.
They laughed a lot and constantly talked, although I could not understand anything they said.

The brush and fallen trees were piling up and I had a desperate
need for a bulldozer. Ted Lewis, our not-yet-present contractor, had
written to me that he had talked with the Public Works Department
and said they might let us use one of their machines. They were crushing
rock to build roads for the American Compound and cleaning up the
remains of the Japanese occupation, and they had several bulldozers.
So, Tuck Wah and I went to the compound and met with Bill Burmeister,
the supervisor of the department. I asked him, "Would it be possible
to get a bulldozer from you?"

Bill was eager to help us, but there was a problem. "We're working five days a week with all our bulldozers," he said.

Tuck Wah Lee said, "What about weekends?"

Bill said, "Well, I guess you could have it on the weekends."

We also needed an operator.

"We have four operators" he said, " and they all live on outer islands and go home to see their families on weekends."

"Do you think I could learn to operate it?" I asked.

I could see his answer on his face. I didn't blame him. I certainly did not look like a bulldozer operator. After a few minutes of hemming and hawing he said: "Let's give it a try." I had never even sat inside a bulldozer before. As a kid back in Mattawamkeag, I used to watch the road crews and had always wanted to be an operator. Now was my chance.

Bill showed me how to start and run the bulldozer. We were on flat ground and maneuvering the blade seemed like a snap. It was fun, just as I always thought it would be. I soon knew how to lower and raise the blade and all of the other stuff a good operator would do.

It was Saturday and I was anxious to show off my new skills and get to work, so off I took, running the machine the two miles down to the to the school site, right down through Mwan Village and onto the school site. Many of the village folk stopped what they were doing to watch. I waved, and they waved back. I was starting to notice that the Trukese respond to emotional actions such as waving, but do not often initiate it.

As I started bulldozing, immediately a large audience gathered to watch. At first I was cautious about not setting the blade too deeply. The ground was always very moist because of the morning rains. I was doing a poor job, but I did make some progress, which gave me a bit of a good feeling.

The next day I got up early on Sunday morning and got back to work with the bulldozer. I was making fairly good progress until I saw Happy New Year leading a group of local men walking toward the site. They looked quite serious. I was so anxious to get work done that I had almost forgot the machine would make far too much noise and would disturb Church service. The Church service was about to start and I had planned to stop when it was time to begin. I figured they had come to nicely remind me of that fact.

I stopped the machine, got off, and approached the men. New Year explained that they were concerned because the Bible indicated work should not be done on the Sabbath. This wasn't just about the noise. I would not be able to operate the machine at all on Sundays.

On Monday Tuck Wah came in from his island and I told him the sad tale. He had an idea. We would go to Chief Petrus to have him decide what to do. We also thought it would be wise to include Wamperon Ernest, the pastor of Logan Church, in our discussion.

Tuck Wah arranged the meeting and we met at the church the following day. We discussed the island's hopes and dreams of building the school. Both Ernest and Chief Petrus agreed that the school was really an act of God for the benefit of all the people of Micronesia. I explained to them why we could not use the bulldozer during the week, but only on Saturdays and Sundays.

Chief Petrus and Wamperon Ernest had a long discussion about it, in their own language. Tuck Wah could understand them, but I could not. I waited for their decision. Finally Chief Petrus turned to us and, speaking in English, told the story of Jesus healing a crippled woman on the Sabbath (Luke 13). When the rabbis questioned his actions Jesus said, "Which of you, having a son or an ox that has fallen into a well on a Sabbath day, will not immediately pull him out?" Since it was God's work we were doing, it would not be sinful to work on the Sabbath. Chief Petrus said, "We've got to build a school. If we have to work on Sunday, we're going to do it."

The volunteer crews continued to clear trees during the week and I continued to work the bulldozer on weekends, but I was not making very good progress on the bulldozer. The rains had been exceptionally heavy for several days. The men were still trying to cut the foliage but even they were discouraged. The rains coming off the higher slopes turned the school site into a mud-collecting field. I could make it run but it was tricky. Whenever I dropped the blade down, particularly in

Rowano bulldozing on the construction site

the muddy jungle if I didn't get it just at the right level, it would dig in, and the bulldozer would go up in the air. I began to think I had gone far from my abilities, but I felt I had no other recourse.

A few weeks after I started operating the bulldozer I came out of my office shack one morning, and there stood a Trukese man, looking as though he had something to say to me. Among many other things I had learned about the Trukese, they never spoke to you until I you gave them permission to do so. Usually a nod of the head or a spoken greeting of some sort was sufficient for them to speak out. I greeted him and that was enough for him to speak to me.

He spoke in mixed English and Trukese. "Me Rowano. Me run bulldozer."

My first thought was, *Thank God*, but my second thought was, *No way!* Tuck Wah had warned me Trukese men were eager to operate machines that were new to them. I was not going to let a Trukese play with my bulldozer, especially since it belonged to the district. I didn't want to have to pay for the destruction of it.

Rowano kept on. "Me run bulldozer. Navy show me how to do."

The Navy taught him! Well, that's a different story. "Let's see what you can do."

He climbed into the operator's seat and started up the engine. What I saw next was amazing. He had that dozer doing tricks I had never ever seen. He could spin the machine around so easily. He could lower and raise the blade, and soon had masses of the wet soil moving right where I wanted it to go.

"You're hired!"

The next few days, regardless of the mud, were a joy. Rowano dug drainage ditches, which took care of most of the excess moisture. He piled up all of the cut debris into burnable piles, and smoothed out two of the major building sites making them ready for construction. Things seemed to finally be going well.

One day I was working in my aluminum office shack while Rowano was clearing an area for a baseball field. Suddenly white smoke billowed around the bulldozer. I saw Rowano, leap from the dozer, land in the thick mud, and run away from the dozer. I thought with dread how much a ruined bulldozer might cost the Mission Board back in New York.

The smoke died away. Rowano returned and started digging in the mud next to the dozer. By the time I got to the machine I saw Rowano dig out a pair of boots from the mud. I knew what they were, his leather boots. (He must have obtained them from the Navy. The Trukese typically only wore "Zoris," a slip-on type of footwear.) There were no laces in Rowano's boots and so when he hit the mud and tried to keep on running, the boots remained stuck in he mud.

Rowano shut off the engine, explaining to me, "Smoke bomb. Japanese."

The Japanese had used phosphorous-loaded bombs to allow troops to move close to the enemy without being seen. We came across many such devices of that nature in our work at the site. We found stacks of 50-gallon metal oil barrels filled with sand that had been arranged as barricades along the shores and up the slopes once used as machine gun mounts by the Japanese.

While bulldozing we also found three German gravesites marked with rough stone markers. The names had worn off, but we could see they were from the years Germany had ruled over the islands from the end of the Spanish American War, 1898 until 1918, the end of World War I. Unfortunately the bulldozer had already damaged the graves by the time we realized what we had unearthed.

We also came across the stone remains of the first mission girls' school in the Truk District, which had been started by Rev. Robert Logan, dating back to 1863.

It seemed like we were archeologists, digging without knowledge as to what we were seeking.

Coconut Legend

To my great relief our contractor, Ted Lewis, finally arrived. Ted had been on a buying cruise, with his wife and two children to purchase the building materials. He went to the Philippine Islands to buy termite-treated lumber, to Honolulu for interior finishing materials, to Taiwan for the windows and doors, and finally to Japan for the cement, hardware, plumbing and sewage materials.

Ted and his family moved into the vacant Quonset hut next to ours at the BOQ site. His two children were near in age to our children, and there was plenty of playing space for the five of them in the plaza right in front of our huts.

With Ted's arrival I was free to begin planning for the operation of the school, which was set to begin in eight or nine months. I needed to start recruiting students. I got to know a few potential students through a young man named Andon Amoraich. He had studied law in America, was working for the Truk Justice Department,[3] and was very active in local church work. He asked me if I would help him start a Christian youth group on Truk. I was willing and

---

3   Ten years later, when the Trust Territory became a new country, The Federated States of Micronesia, Andon became the first Chief Justice of his new country.

eager to do so, not realizing how intense it might become.

I was amazed at how many teenage boys and girls were ready and eager for such an experience. Our first call to the island youth brought out over 50 teenagers from the five villages on Moen Island. We held our meetings on Saturday mornings, with lots of singing, religious classes, and occasional work projects. It was a wonderful opportunity to get to know the teenagers; some of them later became students at my school.

I was eager to start recruiting students from the other islands of Micronesia. I planned a three-month journey and decided to take my family along with me. Geographically, Micronesia covers an area in the Pacific comparable to the contiguous United States. Travel must be either by air or by sea. Airline service made weekly stops at the three districts of The Trust Territory and that would have been the quickest way to travel, but not the most interesting. There were also two cargo ships I could take. The ships brought supplies from the United States and Japan. The islands would send back their primary commercial product, copra, made from coconuts.

There is a great legend about the origin of the coconut, a highly-valued crop among the islands. Many, many years ago when the first people came thousands of miles by canoe to the islands of Micronesia, they found the volcanic-formed islands contained scarcely any food plants. Life was very difficult and it looked like the people might starve to death.

One day an island woman brought forth a newborn baby, but when she took her first look at it she was greatly disappointed. The little baby did not look like her people at all. It had a perfectly round shape and was totally covered with strange brown hair all over its body. She was ashamed of it and wanted to get rid of it. She told her other children to take it into the swamp and bury it so no one could ever see it. The children took the little round hairy ball-shaped baby into the swamp. When they began to dig a hole to bury the baby, the baby spoke to them. They were awe-struck and listened very carefully to what the baby had to say. "Do not bury me, but come every day and bring me

Paul taking a coconut break

some food that I may live. If I live I promise you that I will grow up and provide all of your family with many wonderful things, that they too may live." The amazed children came every day and brought whatever food they could find, but they did not tell their mother.

As the children brought food day after day the little round hairy ball began to grow and to take on a much different shape. It sent little arms down into the swamp. It began to reach higher and higher as it grew. Its hair turned into long green leaves. It grew very, very tall. Then, far up in its top, an amazing thing happened. Small round-shaped, brown, hairy little ones began to form, that looked just like the little baby.

Soon more and more of the same beings began to form and spread out over the islands. The little round-shaped hairy baby that had become great was given a name, the *coconut tree*. The coconut tree provided all the people of Micronesia, through its babies — the coconuts — a delicious creamy milk to drink when they were thirsty, and a very delicious white food inside the crusty shells. It gave them leaves to cover their houses and to make baskets and woven floor mats, and even grass skirts. It provided them with long lengths of wood to build their boats. It provided them with the brown hairs, which, when rolled and twisted together, made excellent ropes and cords for tying their sails to their boats and many other uses. The coconut tree surely lived up to its promises. (I have heard this legend told in several different ways.)

The coconut also provided Micronesia's only cash crop: copra. Local folk would bring their copra to the dock where it would be weighed and paid for on the spot. Eventually it ended up in a coconut oil factory in Japan.

The cargo ships loaded with copra stopped at each district station for three days, which sounded ideal to me and would give me sufficient time to spend with our mission folks as well as the local church folks. The two cargo ships had fitting names: the Pacific Islander and the Gunner's Knot. They were the lifeblood of the islands, bringing in supplies from Japan and the United States, and connecting the many islands on their route.

We had so enjoyed our ship travel from San Francisco to Guam that when the children heard of this trip they were very happy. Of course they would have to take their correspondence courses along with them, but that didn't bother them at all. I didn't realize it at the time, but for them it was an amazing and enlightening experience they never forgot. They proved they could take care of themselves in so many ways, and they were never a burden for their mother or me.

We boarded the Pacific Islander and waved goodbye to our new Trukese friends. We had told the Lewis's about our trip, but in the flurry of planning I had not told our Trukese friends. I learned later they thought we were leaving for good, and we had not even said good-bye to them.

We were assigned first class staterooms of which there were very few as it was mainly a cargo ship. When we boarded we noticed there were quite a few island folk standing on the deck, leaning against the rails with their baskets of food beside them. It was quite obvious they would not be accommodated with staterooms, and they would have to furnish their own food for the trip. They had to sleep on the deck. As I listened to them talking I realized they were not speaking Trukese. I later learned there were nine different languages in Micronesia.

Three days later we landed at the dock in the village of Kolonia on Ponape Island (now know as Pohnpei). Ponape was similar to Truk except that there were more high mountains. Even from the deck of the Pacific Islander we could see some of the well-noted and beautiful Ponape waterfalls. Upon entering the lagoon harbor we were immediately confronted by a massive, very high point of rock known as Sokehs Rock.

Our mission superintendent Harold Hanlin, his wife Mary Ruth, and a small gathering of church officials greeted us at the dock. Our ship was in port for three days, which gave us time to visit the highlights of the island. One of the local church elders acted as our guide, touring us around in very small homemade boat. After an hour's ride we wove our way to an ancient mystical stone village called Nan Madol, meaning spaces between. It is sometimes referred to as the Venice of the Pacific. The village is constructed of massive hexagonal stones, about two feet in thickness, 10 to 20 plus feet in length, and laid upwards of 20 plus feet high. These structures were laid out in the form of streets, which were really canals approachable only by water travel. There is a legend of how a strange group of beings built Nan Madol, a place that has become a worldwide tourist attraction equaling the Pyramids of Egypt.

On Ponape I also became acquainted with Bob Simon, an educational missionary, who directed two schools: the Pastor and Teacher Training School and an elementary school in the village of Ohwa on Ponape. Many of my first students came from that elementary school in Ohwa through the help of Bob Simon.

Our next stop was in the Marshall Islands. I was personally interested in those islands since they were possibly named after one of my ancestors, William Marshall, a British sea captain. We landed on the island of Kwajalein, in the heart of the Marshall Islands. Eldon Buck, the local missionary, and his wife Alice met us at the dock. I thought it was odd that there were no local church folk with them; I learned why later.

The island's natural structure makes it the best seaport of all of the Marshall Islands, and its long stretches of flat land make it an excellent base for aircraft landings, and so Kwajalein was ideal as a base for

American military, scientific, and technology establishments. The native islanders were removed and sent to live on nearby islands. Most of them lived on Ebeye, an island with very little natural growth or resources, thereby the island folk depended entirely on the American compound. Their only means of livelihood was to find employment on Kwajalein, but they were not allowed to reside or even remain overnight on Kwajalein, nor could they make any purchases at any of the shops on the island. The American compound provided transportation morning and night between Kwajalein and Ebeye by a military sea vehicles, known locally as water taxis. Eldon and Alice lived on Ebeye working with the local church leaders and also supervised the local elementary school, from which came several of our students.

My visit at Kwajalein gave me an opportunity to become acquainted with many of the American folk who were part of the congregation of the Protestant Chapel. They were interested in our work and very supportive. When the school opened and incoming students had to pay the tuition fee, several families from the Protestant Chapel adopted students and paid their tuition.

Our return trip back to Truk was equally joyous, perhaps even more so. Our children had made friends with members of the crew. No one was seasick. We had another three days at each stop to enjoy the beauty of the islands and the warmth of the local folk and our stationed missionaries, all of whom we now saw as friends.

The White Elephant

When we returned to Truk I was eager to see the progress Ted Lewis had made at the site. I knew he had planned to retrieve our long-awaited building supplies from a small cargo ship out of Guam.

I soon learned Ted had not yet returned from Guam, but that New Year and the workers had done a fine job preparing the grounds for the buildings. I was pleased at what I saw on the site. They were well under way on the construction of an entrance road. They laid stone bases for the roads and spread gravel topping by hand. The bulldozing had been beautifully done, but the bulldozer was no longer available. They had constructed forms for the reservoir, but we were still waiting for cement for the walls, which would be coming on the ship with Ted.

I refused to become discouraged. Lack of communications made it very difficult. I put my trust in God and I was certain God would not let me down.

Three weeks after my return a small cargo ship was sited coming through the pass. It just had to be ours, I prayed. I hurriedly walked, almost ran to Baker Dock to be there when the ship docked. When it came close enough I was certain I could see stacks of lumber on the decks. The ship, SS Serena, docked, and soon dropped its gangplank. Ted Lewis was the first one to walk down. I never thought I would be so glad to see him.

The next problem we tackled was how to transport the materials to the school site. During my short visit in the Marshall Islands I had shared my vision for the new school with the Americans of the Protestant Chapel in Kwajalein. They were eager to help. The chaplain knew of an abandoned public works delivery van. With some fast thinking and the help of the public works supervisor in Kwajalein, the chaplain loaded the abandoned vehicle onto the Gunner's Knot during the last day of its island stopover. A week after our supplies arrived, the answer to our problem arrived at Baker Dock.

The "White Elephant," formerly a grocery van

Bill Burmeister at the Truk Public Works heard about our van and soon contacted me with an idea. If we removed the van part of the truck, he said, we could make it into a flatbed, a perfect vehicle for moving all of our materials. He offered to have his men do the alteration of the van for free.

Two days later one of the crew drove a white flatbed truck to our school site.

On the doors they had painted in black paint, "The White Elephant." It certainly was an appropriate name. It was our only vehicle and we used it to transport all our materials, including rocks and sand.

The next few days were exciting. The old Japanese road through Mwan Village had not seen such activity since Japanese occupation. Several men from the village volunteered to help us. The SS Serena finished unloading and left our building materials on the dock. The White Elephant was ready and so was Bill Burmeister. Bill was there with a loading machine, without which the task would have taken us many, many days. In just three days we had all of the material delivered to the school site, thanks to Bill Burmeister and the White Elephant. We were ready!

Tuck Wah and I started hiring a permanent crew with the help of the local wamperons. We needed upwards of 40 men. Most men earn their living making copra to sell, and the amount of copra produced in one day would net them around a dollar per day.[4] The wamperons

---

4   I might describe life for the typical Trukese family as "hand to mouth." There were very few opportunities to make money, except a few government jobs and those required some definite skills. However, money was not an absolute necessity. Food was free for the taking as

suggested we pay the men one dollar per day and feed them while they were on the job. We planned for the crew to be on the job early on Monday morning working until five o'clock in the afternoon. The wamperons arranged lodgings in the village for those from other islands, usually with relatives or friends.

I appointed one of the crew from the village to be the timekeeper. He really enjoyed the position, but I had a bit of difficulty teaching him the job. Few adults knew how to tell time. Time was not important to their daily life. They did not have clocks or watches. The crew showed up at different times, some early, some late. No time was kept on them and everyone was happy.

We got to work on completing the reservoir with the arrival of 5,000 bags of cement. The problem was that all we had to mix the cement in was a small hand mixer that could only produce about ten cubic feet at one time. Ted had purchased the sand and crushed rock from the district and I expected he would begin mixing soon. I shortly learned why he was holding off.

About a week after we moved the materials from Baker Dock another ship came in. Ted had not told me anything about another ship so it was a complete surprise to me when the unloading began. The first object they unloaded was a huge gasoline-operated cement mixer, and I mean *huge*! It was followed by two beat-up gray pickup trucks. Next came many eight-foot-long steel columns, and finally several mysterious crates.

When we opened the crates I was amazed at what they contained: desks and office chairs. They were not in the best of condition, but with a few hours of varnishing and adjusting screws they were ready. My opinion of Ted Lewis began to take on new admiration. While in Guam he had befriended some Navy personnel and learned of a seemingly unimportant department known as the Navy Disposal Unit. The Navy replaced old items of all kinds because of wear and tear, and then

---

it grew wild. Fishing was free and also nearby. They rarely needed to buy or wear much clothes. Our crew often wore T-shirts from the American mission box. It was not unusual to see one of the men wearing a T-shirt advertising American beer or a baseball team.

sold them to the public for very low prices. Ted took a good look at the disposal unit and discovered many items we could use in our work. When the officer in charge of the disposal unit heard of our work in Truk he removed all the price tags on the equipment.

For our next big job we had to pour cement walls for the massive reservoir. Our huge cement mixer ran like a dream. We ran a hose from a spring higher up on the slope to have plenty water for the pouring. We borrowed 25 wheelbarrows and a small electric generator from Public Works and strung lights across the forms because we knew it would take ten hours or more to mix and pour all of that concrete. We could work well into the night. We started around noon.

The men were excited. I decided to help and took hold of a wheelbarrow. I clearly remember the look on the men's faces. I guess they had never seen a white missionary doing manual labor before. There was lots of noisy excitement and lots of shouting and laughing among the men. They had never done a job like this. The mixer crew started the engine. The shoveling crew began throwing the sand and rock into the machine. The men were all lined up with their wheelbarrows. I was with them and they kept looking as me as though they thought I probably could not do such hard work. I even wondered myself.

I had not pushed a wheelbarrow since my railroad days when I was in high school. It didn't take long for blisters to form on my hands and my days on the railroad came clearly to my mind. With some ointment and a makeshift pair of gloves, I stayed with it. Several of the men had the same problem, but they also kept on working with a bit of help with their blisters. I developed a great admiration for those men I worked with. I sensed they had the same feeling about me.

Marvel and the kids got the idea of providing refreshments for the crew and served fresh cookies and cold lemonade all night long. (They bought bags of ice from the compound store.)

It seemed as though half of Mwan village gathered around us to help or encourage. We worked long after darkness settled in. It was a joyous and meaningful event in many ways. Finally we finished the reservoir!

Next the crew started construction. It was exciting to see the buildings taking shape. Ted Lewis truly was a builder and the new crew was working out fine. They really enjoyed doing things they had never done before. I thought they looked like children building sand castles on a beach.

Voting Booths

Everyday I walked a good two and a half miles from our BOQ to my office at the school site. I enjoyed walking through the village and chatting with the folks along the way, but the long walk took time away from my work. Marvel and the kids certainly benefitted from the comfortable living at the BOQ. It was close to the supermarket. It had electricity and plumbing, plus a beautiful view across the lagoon. Until the school construction was complete and Ted could turn his attention to building our new home near the school I had to accept this long walk or find some other accommodations. If we moved closer to the school site it would most likely mean we would have to sacrifice all those amenities.

Tuck Wah was concerned about our problem and had taken it upon himself to talk with Chief Petrus about our situation. Chief Petrus had only one solution. His son Caspar had a house in Mwan village, only 200 yards from the school site. We went to look at it, and it was exactly what I had anticipated, a village house, thatched roof and all, no electricity, no running water, no indoor toilet, and no full height walls, only half walls.

The decision had to be mine, but my family always came first with me and I wanted their opinion. The children were excited about it. Marvel was reticent. I certainly was dubious, and yet, I did not want to let Chief Petrus down because I needed his support in everything I had to do in Truk. The decision was made. We moved to the village house.

Our years of family camping in Maine and Vermont were a valuable experience for our new situation. We cooked outside. We carried water from the spring on the school site. There was no electricity, hence no evening lights. Baths were taken in the nearby lagoon. The toilet was another matter.

On our first day after landing in Truk, as we took our first view of Mwan Village, we had noticed small shacks extending out into the lagoon, connected to the shore by two narrow logs as walkways. My daughter Paula asked: "Dad, what are those little houses sticking out over the water?" I had no idea what they were, but I gave them what I thought was a silly answer: "Those are voting booths." They believed me! Just a few weeks before we left home the kids had been following the Goldwater / Johnson presidential election with great interest. They had even gone with me when I went to vote, so they knew what a voting booth was.

It wasn't long after we moved into our new house in the village that we learned what the small shacks were actually used for, because we had to use them ourselves. They became our toilets.

Our only furniture consisted of our mattresses from the BOQ,

A Trukese toilet, or what I jokingly called a "voting booth"

which made it somewhat more comfortable than sleeping on the ground. Trukese village houses had no floors, only hand-woven pandanas carpets. Living in Mwan Village was not as bad as we thought it would be. The local children were intensely curious about us. It was not unusual to wake up in the morning to see them peering over the four-foot high walls at us, and we didn't stop them. Our children soon made friends with the village kids and even began speaking their language.

American people had always lived separately from the village folk before. When the Peace Corps began their work in Micronesia the volunteers who lived with the village folk were more accepted than those who lived in separate quarters. For us, living in the village brought us closer to the village people. Being friendly is truly the best way to live.

Unexpected Help

Not long after we began construction on the buildings a young man came on the site and introduced himself as Bernardo Ronquillo, a foremen from the Philippines. Ted had met Bernardo in the Philippines. When Bernie, as he liked to be called, heard of our work he offered his skills. A relative of Bernie's operated a small cargo ship in the Truk District and even offered to provide Bernie's way to Truk. Bernie was a gift. He was able to work well with the Trukese men and fit well into their way of life. He rapidly learned some bits of the Trukese language, enough for the men to know what he wanted of them.

We had six months until the school opening date and construction was coming along amazingly well, but as usual, there were setbacks. All three major buildings were framed up, roofing completed and ready for inside finishing work. Bernie had certainly proved his worth. The men enjoyed working with him and were very responsive to his leadership. However, Ted's service commitment time was up and he decided not to renew his contract. He was confident Bernie could handle the final finishing touches to the buildings.

I was not especially happy because then I was left to supervise the work in Ted's absence. The plumbing and electrical work on all three of the major buildings had not been done. The generators, which would supply electricity to all of our units, were still in their crates. The interior work required many more weeks of labor. I was so thankful Bernie had come to us.

Bernie and I had to make some very staunch decisions. He thought he could handle the plumbing work, but neither of us knew very much

Bernardo Ronquillo, (Bernie) our construction foreman

about generators or electrical wiring, and we didn't have the funds to seek help from the District.

I have developed a belief that if God expects me to do the tasks set before me, which may seem to be impossible, then God will provide me with the help to do it. I realize this may sound a bit childish, but it has helped me face many difficult tasks. I didn't know how we'd install the electrical systems, or how I'd find time to oversee the work while I tried to put together the teachers and curriculum, but I had faith that somehow it would happen. It was at this juncture when two events came about most unexpectedly.

I was helping prepare concrete forms for the holding tank with the men quite near the village road when I heard men's laughter and loud voices. In just a few minutes the source of the noise came into sight, eight Americans in uniforms were walking down the road toward us. I assumed they were American sailors. Occasionally a Navy ship docked in the harbor on inspection tours, and often the crew was allowed to "let off steam" while in port. They tossed a few beer cans into the ditch and walked toward us. They loudly asked, "What are you doing?" I thought it was obvious. I gave them a brief description,

Crew mixing cement with hand mixer

hoping they would go merrily on their way. They still were quite interested. "Can we help?"

I was worried my workmen might get interested in the beer the Navy men were carrying. I replied again, "I have a good crew. They know what they're doing." Then, without giving it much thought, I told them the only thing I needed was electricity, but we didn't know how to connect the generators.

This last statement brought a laugh out of several of them. "Hey, let us fix them." I still did not trust this rowdy group. I surely did not want them to open the crates with our precious generators and lose some of the parts encased therein. I tried to get them to move on and let us alone to do our work.

One of the men seemed to be quieter than the others and I noticed several stripes on his arm. He spoke up in a quiet manner. "I am the chief of the engine room on the Coast Guard ship that just came in. My crew knows all about generators and we can get them running in a couple of hours."

So they were Coast Guard men, not Navy. They were also good workers. It was a joy to watch them. In a couple of hours our generators

Workers building the administration building

were purring beautifully. Their chief pointed to a tall pole the men had erected and told me, "That pole is ready for you to connect all of your electrical needs for the school." I was so pleased by what he said next. "I and my men are so proud of what you are trying to do for these people who have been put down so many times in the past. We are glad to be able to help you in your work."

Finally, we were making progress on the electrical work, though we were still scratching our heads on how to do the rest. Then, just one week later, I had to make a trip to Guam for supplies. The plane flew in and out only once a week so I decided to kill some time while in Guam with a Navy man by the name of Cecil Cook I'd met there before. He was a very religious man and strongly believed in missionary work in the islands.

Cecil offered to give us a hand when he had some vacation time. He was an older man, probably around 60, and I couldn't think of anything he might be able to do on our job. Instead, I invited him to come to Truk to spend some time with us, and perhaps one of my men would take him fishing out in the lagoon. He said he loved to fish and would definitely come to Truk. He had one more question, "Is there

anything I can do to help you with the electricity on the job?"
Can you imagine my surprise and reaction? Cecil went on to tell me
of his position in the Navy. He was the supervisor of the electrical
maintenance unit in the Navy yard in Guam.

One week after I returned to Truk, Cecil arrived ready to go to
work. He asked me to give him five men to help him. He took charge
of those five men and immediately started to train them how to connect
electrical lines in the three main buildings. It was a joy to watch the
men and their teacher working so beautifully together.

One of my outstanding joys in my work in Truk was to see
American people working together so joyously with the Trukese people.

Island Medicine

The children's correspondence courses were going well. Marvel
had become their teacher and was doing a fine job. Little did she
know at that time that she would become one of the schools regular
teachers when we opened the school.

Our daughter Paula was of high school age and we were concerned
about her having only correspondence courses as her major learning
experience. We had entered her in the local high school, which had been
operating for a very short period of time. She was the only white girl in
the school and she had to walk quite some distance to the school. It did
not seem wise to expose her to any possible harmful situations. The
Mission Board recommended looking for a school in Hawaii. We hated
to send her away from us, but it was important to provide her with a
good education. I wished she could have attended the school I was
building, but it would not be ready for nearly another year, and there
would only be classes for freshmen and sophomores in the beginning.

I had made a connection with Abraham Akaka, the pastor of the
Kahmehameha Church in Honolulu, the oldest mission church in
Hawaii. He suggested we send her to the Mid-Pacific Institute, which
had been established during the early missionary days in Hawaii for

the children of missionaries, who, just like us, were working in many of the far off islands in the Pacific. It was a boarding school noted for its high standards. Our Mission Board would cover the expenses. The Institute required that all students have a "guardian" family located within the State of Hawaii. Abraham Akaka offered his family as Paula's guardian family. Reluctantly we sent Paula off to Hawaii to start her high school education.

Meanwhile, at our house in the village we were still getting accustomed to the lack of facilities most Americans consider absolute necessities. We had to carry our drinking water from a spring on the upper side of our property. Of course, there was no refrigeration, so we drank only very warm water.

Our children followed the local children's style of going bare-footed, except when they wanted to "dress-up" a bit for church, and then they wore the popular local Trukese slip-on footwear known as Zories.

That custom caused us some trouble when our son Alan got an infection in the sole of his foot. The local medical officers, as they were known, determined that he had a stone or shell imbedded in his foot that was causing the infection, and that he should go to the Naval hospital in Guam to have it removed.

The Gunner's Knot was in Truk and getting ready to head for Guam. An American couple we had met was going to Guam for a week vacation. They willingly offered to see that Alan got to the hospital. I also contacted the Navy chaplain in Guam who promised to take care of Alan as long as he had to stay in Guam.

One week later the couple that had taken Alan with them returned with some very bad news. They had checked on Alan's progress and were told that he might have to have his foot removed because the infection had gone wild.

It is hard to explain how difficult communications were in Micronesia. There was no island-to-island telephone service. Short-wave radio, controlled by the district offices, was the only way to make quick contact with anyone, and that was not always available. There was nothing we could do until a plane left for a return trip to Guam.

The Marshall family visits fellow missionaries Eldon and Alice Buck and their family (center) on the Marshall Islands. Paula and Alan on far left. Marvel Marshall on far right. January, 1964

Fortunately we only had to wait one more day. Marvel took the flight to Guam to see our son.

Several weeks later the flight from Guam landed. I waited with my fingers crossed and my hopes high. The steps went into place, the plane door opened, and out stepped Alan on both natural feet, with his hand in his mother's, and his usual big grin on his face.

In our "advanced" western culture when something goes wrong with our bodies we simply push a button, so to speak, and get what we want. The Micronesians have developed their own ways of meeting up with life's difficulties, and I had the good fortune to be on the receiving line of some of that knowledge.

During the construction of the school due to the lack of heavy machinery we relied primarily on manpower to get the job done. I was helping my work crew place a very large timber into place when my back suddenly disagreed with what I was doing, and as a result I could not straighten up without considerable pain.

My only thought was to head to the district hospital in the village of Nandaku. I had an x-ray and the doctor told me the good news

Family of Fango and Irene Bonochou in Mwan Village. Fango was crew foreman
of Mwan village men

that nothing was broken. He recommended I fly to Guam for special
chiropractic treatment—muscle and bone replacement—was the term
the district doctor used.

The jeep ride back to my shack in Mwan Village was painful enough
to make me realize a 600-mile plane ride to Guam would be more than
I could withstand. Plus, I'd have to wait another whole week for the
plane to Guam. At least the doctor had given me some pain pills.

My next-door neighbors were Fango and Irene Bonochou, and
their children. It probably was God's intent for us to be placed next to
such a wonderful family. Fango was my village foremen and knew all
the workers by first name. They all held the highest respect for
him. If I had to choose only one person to help me through those
difficult times, I would have chosen Fango.

A couple of days later I was lying on my mat in our shack when
Fango returned from work. I heard his voice outside the shack, "Mista
Massen, Irene and me, fix back."

Fango and Irene then had me lay flat on my stomach with my arms
and legs stretched out as far as possible. It was painful, but I was able

to do it. She started at my hands and he started at my feet, and they began massaging everything, fingers, and toes, followed by all muscles and bones, both moving at the same pace very slowly. They both reached my waist at the same time. They gave one last heavy coordinated push, and my pain was gone! I felt totally relieved.

I told this story to my present-day chiropractor and he laughed and said, "I think I missed that procedure in chiropractic school."

Too often we of the "civilized world" do not understand the minds of those who have been deprived of the "intellectual world." Many island folk believe that certain persons are gifted as healers, and those who are so gifted must be treated very carefully in their day-to-day encounters.

Where Are My Teachers?

I had no telephone, no short-wave radio contact. My only means of communication was through the mail, which came and went once a week. It could take three weeks to receive an answer. The Mission Board promised to help me find teachers, but so far all I had was Marvel and myself. I needed a basic staff of six to eight teachers. I kept asking, "Will I have enough teachers?" and "When will they arrive?"

The Mission Board found Bill Petry, a mathematics teacher for our new school. At the time he was working at a mission elementary school on the Marshall Islands. I contacted Bill by slow mail and asked him to come to Truk sooner to help with the final building work. Bill accepted and came on the next Pacific Islander ship run.

Bill was a very likable person and I knew I would enjoy having him with me. I wanted him to help Bernie with the men. Bill said he knew nothing about building construction, but I convinced him that all he had to do was to wear white clothes and encourage the men in their work. White clothes in Micronesia meant authority. Bill's quality of love for everyone, which made him a good missionary, worked well with the men.

Mizpah High School

Bob Simon, our missionary on Ponape, found another teacher for me, a young Ponapean man by the name of Danny Leopold, who had gone to college in California and recently returned home seeking a teaching position. Bob approached Danny with the Mizpah offering. Danny was very willing to come to Mizpah if he could bring his wife. My very quick responding letter was: "Yes, send him and his wife right along." They arrived on the next Gunner's Knot run. My office in the small aluminum building had just enough room to serve as a temporary home for two people. I assigned that to Danny and his wife.

Under Bernie's leadership the construction of the teacher's apartments moved along much faster than I had even hoped. It was an exciting time. Soon we'd have electricity, running water—all the amenities of modern living once again.

With the added help of Cecil Cook and Bill Petry the work was moving along at a fast pace, and it looked like another month of that kind of progress would open up the teacher's quarters for at least two or three of our teachers and families.

My school material orders, via Japan, were arriving every day. Classroom chairs and student desks came first. Ranges and refrigerators and fans for the apartments followed. (Fans were a real necessity due to the

Principal Paul Marshall in his office

temperatures that not only ranged high through the days, but abated only a little during the night.) Textbooks by the boxes began arriving even before the classrooms were finished. The chapel on the first floor of the administration building became a temporary storage room.

As I look back on those days I find it difficult to comprehend how we were able to perform so many different actions. And yet, I recall those days as some of the happiest and most exciting ones. I think it was because we were approaching our final goal, the opening of the school.

I was beginning to feel more comfortable now that I had four teachers to start with: Bill Petry to teach mathematics, Danny Leopold for social studies, Marvel for music, and I would teach science. I had hoped for a home economics teacher but would have to hold off on that subject till we found someone.

Meanwhile, we set a date for the school dedication ceremony for July 16th. We sent notices to all of the outlying villages and mission stations. After several days of decorating the building with palm branches and native flowers we were ready. Many noted dignitaries attended the ceremony as well as many people from the local villages of Moen Island. We cooked several small pigs over coconut fires on spits in the Trukese fashion. There were large quantities of bananas, papayas, drinking coconuts, and specially-prepared breadfruit dishes. There was plenty of food for everyone. Many of the dignitaries gave wonderful blessings and prayers and dedication speeches, saluting the wonderful work of the local men and all of those who had given so much of their energies and skills to the beginning of this new school.

With the celebration aside I still needed at least two more teachers to reach my minimum goal, and there was only a month and a half left before school would start. One of the problems was that the board was experiencing some challenges recruiting teachers to the mission field. The Peace Corps was quite new to the world. It was founded in 1961 with the help of Robert Kennedy. Thousands of volunteers had been trained and sent off to countries around the world that needed help providing education, sanitation, medical care, and other needs. It had similar goals and programs, but volunteers for the mission field had to sign up for five-year terms, while the requirement for the Peace Corps was only three years. However, the Peace Corps was willing to share some of their volunteers with us.

I contacted the Peace Corps office to see about finding a teacher, particularly someone to teach home economics. I hoped they would send a young person with lots of energy to fill not only a teaching post but also to be an active guide for my students' personal lives. The Peace Corps welcomed my request heartily. They had a new volunteer and were having some difficulty placing her because of her age. She was 72 years old, the oldest acceptable age for the Peace Corps. My joyous eagerness faded somewhat. My teachers' apartments were three stories up, meaning she would have to run up and down several times a day and also in the night. I had only a few weeks before the students were due to arrive and so I hesitantly signed on the "oldest Peace Corps volunteer," Sarah Pick, as our home economics teacher.

I was also invited to visit the Peace Corps training site to talk about our work and goals at Mizpah. A group of Peace Corps volunteers were stationed on Udot Island, one of the high islands in the Truk lagoon, for a month-long on the job training to learn basic language skills and experience living with local folk.

I took my small mission boat, crossed 30 miles of the lagoon to Udot Island, and was quite surprised to find 100 volunteers there awaiting my presentation. They were all sitting on the ground and looked like a collection of college students. I scanned their heads for one with white hair, but none could I see. Sarah, at 72 years of age, surely must have a white head of hair, I thought. I was relieved to think she must have decided not to come because I had told her advisors the living quarters for my teachers were on the third level and might be too difficult for her to use several times a day.

I lectured and answered questions for nearly an hour. As I was saying my goodbyes I caught sight of a small white head bobbing up and down from the rear ranks. The first person to rise was the one with the white head waving her hand. It had to be Sarah Pick. This tiny, but healthy-looking, white-haired person came trotting right toward me.

As soon as I heard her, "Mr. Marshall, I am Sarah Pick," I changed my mind right then and there. She wasn't the mousy quiet person I had expected. Her confidence was evident right away. I could see that she would work out fine.

Sarah and I were getting ready to leave Udot for our trip across the lagoon to Truk when a young man approached me. He introduced himself as John Gundale and said he wanted to teach at our school. I could hardly believe what was happening. I spent the next hour listening to John lay out his life story, and even before he was through I knew I had another teacher. John had a good college background in social studies, came from a religious family, and was interested in choral singing and choral leadership. Sarah had been with him in the preliminary Peace Corps training and just kept nodding her head while we were talking. I knew what she was trying to do.

My little boat was somewhat overloaded on the way back to Truk with two more passengers and their luggage. Yet the return trip was an exceedingly happy one. With only two weeks before school I had my six teachers.

Does Anyone Know of a Cook?

O ur school had a kitchen and dining room on the first floor level of the administration building thanks to Bernie and his crew, including a good-sized freezer and two refrigerators. I spent many frantic hours planning our meal program, another task in which I had very little experience. The U.S. Department of Agriculture could supply us with vegetables and frozen meat. Other missionaries, Bob Simon and Eldon Buck, advised me to include both native and American foods.

I negotiated with locals to supply us with fish and bananas, which were plentiful, and occasionally taro, a starch-based root that when boiled and mashed becomes the basic staple food of most Pacific Islanders. In Hawaii it is called "poi." Another island food commonly eaten by the local folk is "breadfruit," a product of very large trees that grow quite high in the mountains and is somewhat difficult to obtain. Taro on the other hand grows in the lower parts of the islands and is easy to obtain. I also set a goal to raise our own pigs and chickens, something we achieved in our second year of operations, thanks to Tom Chilton, our agricultural and mechanical arts teacher, who joined us the first year.

We had the food, but we did not have a full-time cook. I knew I could get a few locals to be cook aides, and I expected students to assist in cleaning tasks, but I badly needed someone with cooking skills. Our meager staff of teachers took turns preparing meals while I continued to search for a qualified person to take over. It looked on the verge of hopelessness!

Word got around of our need. I am not a believer of miracles, *per se*, but I have always had a sense that God provides in mysterious ways.

One week before the opening of our school, a Trukese man came to my door. He introduced himself as Ticara. He spoke fairly good English. Before I could ask him what was his reason for coming to me, he said very simply: "I am a cook. I was trained by the Navy. I will cook for Mizpah."

I couldn't believe it was happening again. Ticara not only knew how to prepare American-style meals, but he could also prepare native island foods. He was especially talented in cooking stuffed whole pigs on a spit over an open fire, a feast we celebrated many times at Mizpah in the coming years.

Students Arrive

Missionaries around Micronesia sent us letter after letter filled with exciting news. They had tested and approved of nearly 30 students for our freshman class. We all were so eager to meet our first students, children from a distinctively different culture than our own. We began to wonder how they would receive us? How should we relate to them? I was the only one with any professional teaching experience.

There were concerns about the tuition fee, $150 per year, an amount that might seem ridiculously low to an American, but was a considerable amount of money for most Micronesians. I had been told the average Micronesian family's annual income was in the vicinity of $200 per year. I assured our missionaries I would not turn down any student whose family could not meet the tuition fee. When I was preparing to enter the mission field before I left the States many of my church friends offered to help in any way they could. I felt now was the time to seek their aid. I sent many letters sent off to them and was happy to find quite a few friends who wanted to help with the students' tuition fees.

Bernie and our crew were pushing hard for the finish. It was always a joy to watch them give out their best. Our classroom interiors were completed. Our student desks and chairs, typewriters, teaching paraphernalia, even fans for our rooms, had all arrived but still needed to be unpacked.

My family and I felt like we had been living out of our suitcases for over a year, but it had not seemed like a real burden to us. With only one month to go our apartment was finally ready! In a way we hated to leave our village home as we had made many friends there.

Mizpah students

But to have hot and cold running water, a real shower, refrigerator, and electricity—what American can turn down such luxury?

Bill Petry moved into Tuk Wah and Alice's old aluminum hut, and Danny and his wife moved into one of the nearly-finished teacher apartments. Everyone was happy and ready to go.

Then I received a letter informing me that 32 students and one Marshallese churchman were aboard the Pacific Islander headed for Truk. I was not particularly happy with that news. I had hoped to have two more weeks. A week later the boat landed at Baker Dock.

It is difficult to describe the feeling I had seeing my first students. They all looked so young, and they were, mostly 14 and 15 year olds, away from their home islands for the first time. Most toted their belongings in handmade cloth bags. The girls were dressed in their remodeled "Mother Hubbard" style of dresses and the boys wore shorts or long pants and shirts, many of which certainly looked like they had come out of a mission box. All the students sported *mwaramwas,* a ring of flower blossoms around their heads, much like the leis of Hawaii.

I had to figure out how to transport 32 students and their meager belongings to the school. The jeep could carry, at most, six people, so I enlisted two taxis, which on Truk meant an open pick-up truck with wooden plank seats along each side of the body. As we drove along the

Mizpah students

road to the school the students were excited but also rather quiet. If it had been a group of young Americans you probably could have heard them a mile away. Micronesian young folk always seemed much quieter in showing their excitement. My heart went out to them. Those youngsters would be in my care for the next four years. I could see that I had my hands full.

For several days our main activity was to get acquainted. We wanted our students to feel comfortable with us, not just as teachers, but also as friends. We would all be living together, night and day. As we opened the doors of Mizpah for those eager young folks I saw them as my children, as part of my family. I saw myself, not as their ruler, but as their father, a different concept then they had known on their islands. I encouraged my teachers to be more than just teachers, but also fathers, mothers, brothers, and sisters, because we lived very closely together like a family. I appointed two teachers to serve as the Dean of Boys and Dean of Girls. My Dean of Boys once said to me that he felt more like a father to the boys than a dean. My answer was: "Great! Keep it up!"

Through those days before classes started we played games and sang songs, took walks together along the beach and even went swimming a few times.

Those few days set the theme for how we would operate our school.

The MV Banana

At Mizpah High Tom Chilton taught industrial arts, agriculture, and mechanical arts. Tom had originally been appointed to mission work in Africa. When he discovered he was headed to a goat farm in Africa he was extremely happy to choose Micronesia as his alternative. I am so glad he made that choice. There seemed to be no end to the skills Tom taught his Mizpah boys.

Tom had studied agriculture, particularly vegetable gardening. Very soon after classes began Tom and his students planted small garden patches around the campus. Next, Tom brought carpentry skills to the students. The island folk had a history of boat building, but a lack of materials inhibited their knowledge of modern building materials. They certainly had little experience with electrical and mechanical tools. Soon Tom had the students working with modern tools. He taught them to operate and repair outboard motors as well as the school's two huge electrical generators, both valuable skills for island culture.

An elderly Trukese man named Essen came to me shortly after Tom started teaching carpentry. His English was quite good and he said he also spoke Japanese. As a young man he had been sent to Japan to learn to build modern boats for the Japanese. When he returned to Truk he decided he wanted to teach these skills to his own people, especially the young folk, and so I set him up to teach with Tom. Essen actually became one of our best unsolicited teachers. It was such a joy to see how Tom and Essen melded together, joining the skills of two very different cultures. I often would quietly drop in on them and their boys. As I watched them putting their skills together I could not help but wonder why all of us, the world over, were not able to do the same.

Tom, Essen, and the boys got to work on a boat they named the MV Banana (MV meaning motor vehicle). The MV Banana was not a small boat. It was built to carry 40 to 50 students and teachers.

As I watched them work I grew concerned about how I would be able to pay for two 50-horsepower engines that were necessary to propel the boat around the lagoon. I had already received a warning from the

Launching the MV Banana boat Mizpah

Mission Board that the funds for building the school were almost exhausted. I looked over my list of churches and friends whom I had already approached heavily for assistance in many ways. They had all responded faithfully and I did not want to overload them. An idea came to me. What if I approached the Evinrude Company itself and told them the story of building Mizpah High School and the great need for motors for our boat? Perhaps they would at least give me a discount. I sent a letter off to them immediately and in just two weeks I received their answer. They were shipping two Evinrude 50-horsepower engines to Truk, due to arrive within a month and at no charge!

When the MV Banana was complete we held a launching ceremony. It was a day of great joy. The entire student body and teachers placed their hands on it, singing and shouting, they carried it down to the docking area, a special area we had prepared weeks before launching. With lots of singing and tossing flowers we made several runs up and down the lagoon.

Every Sunday morning the MV Banana carried students to one of the islands nearby. Our band and choir played for their morning worship service, and a deliciously prepared island feast always rewarded us afterwards. The MV Banana brought much joy to the island communities and us.

Tom and Essen also guided the boys in building their very own "sea chests." Sea chests were made of wood, could contain most any island person's entire belongings and were suitable for the frequent boat travel that Micronesian life required. The chests were patterned after the sea chests of early New England whalers. Every boy at Mizpah High School built his own chest thanks to Essen and Tom.

Tom and all of our teachers became friends and counselors to the children, teaching them by their own actions what a good life can be had in the new world if all of us care about each other as we care about ourselves.

Sarah Pick

Before the Missionaries came to Micronesia, the women wore grass skirts. The Missionaries taught the women that it was a sin to expose their bodies and that was the beginning of dresses. After that, Micronesian women began making their own clothing, which consisted mainly of dresses and skirts. Most of the sewing had to be done by hand, a very slow and tedious task. The first Missionaries introduced the treadle sewing machine, but very few islanders could afford to own one.

Sarah Pick

Mizpah Marching Band

We purchased non-electric treadle sewing machines to teach our girls a skill that would be important in their future lives. Not only would they be capable of making their own clothing but also for their children and their husbands.

When Sarah Pick volunteered for the Peace Corp she had no idea she would end up teaching home arts in an American-style high school. I had no idea that I would end up with a teacher who had never taught a class before. She had been a farmer's wife for most of her adult life. However, I soon learned she was an ideal candidate for the job. Her sweet and happy nature was a gift both to my staff and to all of the girls who lived in the dorm with her. Most importantly, she knew how to sew. She could teach our girls a skill that would be with them for the rest of their lives, and even though their future income may be quite small, they would be able to provide all of the clothing needs for their families.

I started a school band, and by the second year we had 30 students, all playing instruments, and ten baton twirlers. We practiced every day in the chapel and Sarah would often sit and listen. One day after practice she approached me and asked if the band would ever play for the public. My response was, although I thought they were musically ready to do so, I had hoped we might have uniforms so they would look more "band like."

Sarah then asked, "Why don't they have uniforms?"

I answered, "We have no money to purchase them and I don't know when we might have any."

Sarah quickly responded, "After my husband died I owned a sewing shop in Salem, Oregon and I specialized in making band uniforms." Imagine my surprise! Then she asked me to sketch a design for the uniforms. The next day she brought me a complete uniform made exactly in my design. She offered yet another wonderful suggestion. "If you could purchase the materials I would love to teach the girls in my sewing class the art of making band uniforms."

The next day I bought enough varied colored cloth from the Truk Trading Post to make 30 uniforms, and in just 20 days Sarah and her sewing class girls presented our band with beautiful new uniforms.

Two days later when a contingent of legislators from the United States landed at the airport, the band marched onto the field to greet them with joyful music, wearing their brand new uniforms. Thanks to Sarah Pick, the 72-year-old Peace Corps volunteer whom I at first thought might be a burden to us. I learned that age has no limits in the sharing of gifts. Sarah was like a mother and grandmother to our students and all of us teachers too.

Marvel

Mizpah Mixed Chorus under the direction of Principal Marshall

I am so grateful for the support and presence of my wife, Marvel, especially for the months of difficulty when we lived in a native shack, awaiting the construction of our new housing. But I especially praise her for her gifts when the time came to open classes of our new school in Micronesia.

I planned for a complete business curriculum for the school, which would include classes in typing, bookkeeping, business administration, and such, but I had no teachers for those classes. My wife Marvel had only a high school education and had begun a nurses training course but left it only half completed when we left for the Mission field. I asked her if she thought she might be able to teach business courses until I could obtain a fully-qualified business teacher, and her answer was: "I will try."

A few months before our first students arrived, a parcel of school-books came. Immediately Marvel set studying their contents, especially the teachers' manuals. When school opened she was nervous, but ready. Every one of our new students were eager to take the business courses,

Marvel Marshall teaching type writing

especially the typing classes. Within just a few weeks I could see she made an excellent teacher.

We also had a very important need for a school nurse. Marvel, because of her half-year's nurses training course, became our school nurse and a very efficient one. She was much needed, especially when our entire school came down with a hepatitis infection, and there was only one doctor available on the island. Marvel was available for all of our students, night and day through the infection time.

One more gift Marvel brought with her to Micronesia was her skill in music. Marvel became the organist for our daily chapel services, and our accompanist for all of our student choirs. We brought a piano with us from our own home in New England, knowing we would need one to accompany our choruses and choirs.

We also discovered there was a high demand among the many new developing churches for people who could play portable organs. Many churches donated portable organs to the school and we made it possible for all students who were interested to take organ lessons. Most of them were eager to learn, and somehow Marvel found time to teach many students to play the organ.

We were so blessed to have such a person as Marvel on our team.

Special Teachers

During my four years as the Principal of Mizpah High School I was fortunate to have many outstanding teachers. All of them were very special to me and to their students. I have already told you of Tom Chilton, my wife Marvel, and Sarah Pick, the oldest Peace Corps Volunteer.

There was John Gundale, another Peace Corps volunteer who brought many skills with him and became not only a wonderful teacher but also a leader of outdoor activities as well as choral groups of both boys and girls. Bill Petry, a happy, always smiling, loyal young man, one I could count on for just about anything that I needed done. Then there was Julia Rahib, a young lady from the far-away country of Jordan, teaching English-as-a-second language and also bringing to us her skills in artistic stage productions. Julia later became Mrs. Bill Petry. Our Home Economics teacher, Marlene Campbell, years later reflected on her teaching experience at Mizpah and how it changed her life in so many ways. Marlene had no experience in professional teaching before coming to Mizpah, but she very soon became an excellent teacher. She was always a very caring and loving example for all of her students.

I would be remiss if I did not reflect on the skills and the loving work of the two Micronesian teachers who came on to my staff. First was Danny Leopold, a Ponapean young man who had just completed a Mission scholarship in the States. Because he was Micronesian, his presence provided "local" guidance for all of the students, who went to him first with concerns before they came to the rest of us. The other young man, Aichy Sos, of Truk, also had completed a Mission scholarship. He had a love of books and libraries. He became fascinated with his westernized college studies. His interests helped Mizpah to have an outstanding school library.

My ultimate praise and thanks goes out to all of those unusual teachers, all of whom had not professionally prepared for teaching, and yet provided the pathways for our Mizpah students to become

"Christian leaders of their new world." They gave their unusual gifts so freely and so lovingly to the young boys and girls who were fortunate to have been a part of the Mizpah Experience.

Love Sticks and Other Culture Lessons

Our students came from islands scattered across Micronesia that were a part of the U.S. Trust Territory, including the Marianas Islands, Marshall Islands and Caroline Islands. They each brought with them their own distinctive island customs and languages. Those differences separated the students somewhat, but at the same time, they appeared to enjoy learning each other's ways.

In the evenings at Mizpah we encouraged an exchange of customs with cultural performances. Costumes were very important and varied from district to district. Under the direction of Sarah Pick and Marlene Campbell, our two excellent home arts teachers, the girls made their own special dresses and grass skirts. The boys wore somewhat more exposed costumes for their dances.

Each island group has their form of dancing. For the Micronesians each dance expresses a spiritual experience and carries a deep significance for their people. These sorts of dances have become quite popular and are exciting to watch, as they require a great deal of skill. The meaning of these dances has become somewhat lost since dancing in that part of the world is now mostly a tourist attraction.

The boys commonly used various types of sticks in their dances. Stick dancing requires a very challenging skill, not easily attained. Their dances often demonstrated conflicts between opposing forces from the past. The girls' dances usually emphasized bodily movements, similar to the well-known hula dance in Hawaii, although different in style.

I have always been interested in all forms of dancing and especially what is known in the good old USA as country dancing, inherited from our European ancestors. Observing how much our students enjoyed their dances I was anxious to teach them the art of country dancing. I even had several country-dance records with me from Vermont. Our students loved this new form of dancing, and we, teachers and students, were all truly enjoying ourselves every Saturday night for a few weeks. I had no thoughts about how we might be disturbing our neighbors in the village, although we did have the record player turned up high enough so that everyone could hear the music well.

One Sunday afternoon, Alphonso, the Mwan Village wamperon, accompanied by several other wamperons, paid us a visit. I was pleased to see them and I thought they were there to make a friendly visit. Alphonso politely asked me if he could talk about the school. He began with words of praise of what we were accomplishing. Then he brought up the real reason for their visit. They were concerned about the country dancing because it allowed the boys and girls to hold each other in their arms. They thought that was an evil thing to do. Apparently, some early missionaries taught that close personal contact among young folk was evil and something that would lead to disaster.

I knew I would not be able to convince the wamperons differently and assured them that we would cease that activity. I was concerned that if I went against the wamperons I would lose their support, which meant a great deal to Mizpah's future. I learned early on to accept the somewhat strange ways of the local people. I believe they thought many of our ways were also odd.

I wish Margaret Mead, noted especially for her book *Coming of Age In Samoa*, had done some research in Micronesia. If ever I am again called to work in a culture very different from my own, I certainly will do a study of the people and their culture long before I go to live and serve with them.

In 1963 when I first arrived in Micronesia I observed entire Trukese families, including mother, father, children, husbands of married daughters, and grandchildren, living and sleeping in one-room partially open structures with thatched roofs. No beds. The ground floor was covered only with woven mats. The bedroom was open to geckos (small green lizards who love to chew around the toes of the family at night), flies of all sorts, and especially mosquitoes, and an occasional bird that got lost during its night flight.

My Trukese friend, Andon Amaraich, whom I turned to whenever I needed any information about anything Trukese, warned me about the sexual activities of young Trukese teenagers. Girls sometimes would show up pregnant, a deep concern for the parents. Already there would be several babies and children living in the family circle. When we lived in Mwan Village I noticed the very young children calling out "mama" to any of the ladies of the house, and I had difficulty determining who was who's mother or who was who's child. Andon explained that it really didn't matter very much as they all lived closely together and they all took care of the children. He also added an interesting thought: if a mother could not nurse her child one of her sisters could often take care of feeding the baby.

Boy-girl relationships in Micronesia, especially in Truk, were quite different than those in the United States. There were no opportunities for them to be together openly. Parents were protective, hoping to keep their daughters from becoming pregnant until after marriage. Yet, a peculiar custom existed so that boys and girls could meet secretly at night. In Truk a teenage boy would carve a special design on two sticks, a long stick and a short one. He would wear the short stick in is hair. If a girl was interested in him she had to make note of the special design on the boy's stick in his hair so she could recognize it. At night when the family had all gone to sleep together in their one-room hut, the boy would approach. Somehow he had to find out just where the girl was sleeping. (I never learned just how that was done.) He would then push his love stick through the wall thatch, poking the girl. If she recognized the design and was interested she would pull it in, which meant that soon she would meet the boy outside. If she did not recognize the design on the stick, she would push the stick back out, and the boy would go away before her papa awoke.

Love sticks, fortunately because of our solid walls and watchful faculty, did not work at Mizpah. However, I was still concerned for my students. The parents were deeply concerned about their teenagers living far from home. Mizpah students were exposed to a very different style of living from that of their home villages. Our boys and girls dormitories were well separated, and our teachers' apartments were located on the top level of both the girls' and boys' dorms. Each dorm had a curfew bell, and our evening programs left very little time for boy-girl relationships. The system worked very well, for the most part, during all of my time at Mizpah.

We did have a problem one night, though, with a group of boys sneaking out at night. Three of our boys somehow managed to elude the dean of boys one night. They walked into the village and came across a man who sold them beer. They returned to the dorm late at night and woke up most of the boys in the dorm as well as the dean. I was called from my sleep and spent the next two hours quieting things down. I also found out who sold them the beer.

I took the name of the beer seller to the District Administrator to see if he could prevent this situation from happening again. He knew the village man who worked for the District super-market. While ordering items for the market he also managed to set aside a substantial order of beer for himself, which he decided to sell in the village, illegally of course without a license. Before the take-over by the United States, most Micronesians could not afford to buy alcohol. The U.S. Navy brought cheap beer to the island and some Micronesians picked up this new habit.

I warned the boys that if they snuck out to go to the village again I would have to expel them from Mizpah, a task I would have hated to do, as these boys were outstanding in every other way. Fortunately it was the one and only event of its kind that occurred at Mizpah. The District Administrator very soon put a stop to the illegal sale of beer in Mwan Village.

Future Leaders

The people of Micronesia had never been free to govern themselves before. For thousands of years world super powers dominated these islands, seeking riches only for their own good. After World War II they were released from the Japanese, and the United Nations decreed Micronesia was to prepare for democratic self-government. I believed the new direction for the Micronesian people depended on their youth.

My students had been taught to obey their elders and rulers "or else." They were not allowed to think or make decisions. At Mizpah, those rules were put aside so we could encourage a new kind of thinking. The Student Senate was one of the first programs we started to help teach the students about self-government. I likened it to the American legislative process: "for the people, by the people," so everyone had a say.

Pre-election time was the most exciting. Students delivered speeches telling why they thought they should be chosen to serve on the Senate. I was amazed at how many students took part in that activity. The week before elections the entire student body sat and listened to four one-hour sessions of speeches. The results were overwhelming. We all got to know one another in a much closer connection. For the first time in their lives they were able to express their personal beliefs and have others listen to them.

The first order on the Senate table was to establish a "Code of Living," a title I suggested because I did not want it to seem like laws, which, when broken, would lead to punishments. (I sensed that the early Christian missionaries who had come before had put too much emphasis on obeying the Ten Commandments, which is not much different from obeying a super power, and not enough on Christ's teachings of love.) I wanted our school to offer an example of how to live a Christian way of life through love, honesty, and caring, not just rules.

We gathered in the chapel with one purpose, to draw up the elements of the Code. There were representatives from each class, with an equal number of boy and girl representatives. Teachers acted as

Mizpah girl's volleyball game

consultants, but the students made all of the final choices. The Code may have sounded much like the Ten Commandments, but the results we hoped to achieve were very different, and punishment was not to be the result. For me, it was a joy to see the way my teachers and students showed such respect for each other. The Senate became one of the most meaningful activities at Mizpah.

Our students would certainly be required to have new skills in their "new world," including typewriting. Marvel did an excellent job conducting that subject, and the students were always excited to attend her typing class. Soon they were typing essays for their English classes and it seemed as if the air was filled with the click-clack of typewriters.

I also wanted the students to learn the value of self-expression and to share the news of what they were accomplishing; hence the *Mizpah Missile* began! First, the students organized the Press Club and created positions for an editor, an assistant editor, reporters, typists, and artists. The *Missile* advisor, Miss Julia (Petry) Rahib, our wonderful gift from the far off Middle-East country of Jordan, put her skills to developing a school program that reached far beyond the walls of Mizpah. Soon

Paul Marshall teaching a science class

the Press Club staff began producing a high-quality biweekly issue. Our postage bills ran quite high as issues were sent out to District offices throughout the Trust Territory and to any of the students' parents who had a mailing address. (Postal services were just beginning in Micronesia, so there were very few family mailboxes.) Copies of the *Missile* were also sent to individuals and American churches that provided tuition or support to our school.

All students were encouraged to write articles for print, especially articles relating to their own family background and family cultures. Occasionally a particular topic was selected, such as: "How Your World Is Changing." It was amazing how many students eagerly presented opinions on each subject. The real joy in publishing the *Missile* was reading what was happening in the minds of those top-grade youths of Micronesia. For the first time in their lives they were allowed and encouraged to realize their own importance in this world.

In addition to the Senate and the *Missile* I knew a debate club could teach our students many valuable lessons. During my teaching days in Vermont I directed the debate team at Vergennes Union High, and we won many debates. I could hardly wait to form a debate team at Mizpah.

There were two other schools in the area we could compete with, the Truk Territory High School and Xavier High School, a Catholic school considered to be the highest quality high school in Micronesia. I wanted our team to win over Xavier. But more than winning I wanted to help prepare my students to become the Christian leaders of Micronesia.

I taught my students that as leaders they would have to convince their audience what was best for them and all the people of Micronesia. Debating requires you to give an honest and firm presentation of your beliefs. The art of speaking to an audience in a clear and concise manner must convince the listener to believe what you profess.

My students were excited about debating, having an opportunity to express themselves, and have someone listen to them. Preparing for our first debate against Xavier High was a bit scary for them, and I knew it. I planned a mock debate right at Mizpah, having the teachers as judges, which helped them to practice and develop their confidence. Our teachers helped the students prepare their pro and con presentations. One question remained, "Are we ready?"

The debate was held in the Territory hall. The district administrator chose the topic of the debate: "Democracy or Communism." I was amazed at the number of people who attended, teachers from Xavier, teachers from Mizpah, Chief Petrus, several wamperons, and quite a few local folk, who stood outside, but could still hear the debaters.

I remember thinking, "These students, from both schools, will become the leaders of their new world."

The applause was great on both sides. I could feel the tension in the hall. The presentations were strong on both sides. I remembered going through this phase with my students in Vermont, but I never thought I would be doing the same thing in a far off place called Micronesia.

At the conclusion of the debate the district administrator gave a long talk praising both sides. Would he ever get to the final announcement?

"And the winner of the debate is...Mizpah High School of Micronesia."

I think this achievement opened the eyes of my students to a different world, and they knew they'd be an integral part of it.

The Road Home

It was 1968. After five years of living and working with the Micronesians my term serving as a missionary was up and I came to a split in the road. I had to decide if I should stay another five years or return home; it was not an easy choice. I felt good about the work I had done. I had accomplished my goal of building and conducting a modern American-style high school. In the eyes of the district administrator our school was "the finest school in Micronesia." We had an outstanding faculty. Our students were fine capable young men and women headed for college studies. I even felt my goal of preparing Christian leaders for their new world was well on its way to being accomplished. I had experienced the joy of helping these people take control of their lives for the first time in their history.

Again, Mr. Robert Frost, *which road should I take?*

I wondered: *What will happen to Mizpah High School if I leave? Can the Mission Board find a capable replacement to steer the entire operation?* The board had already shown that getting staff for a five-year term in a far off patch of islands 3,000 miles from the American mainland would not be an easy task.

For myself, I was concerned about finding a job in the education field back home. My wife wanted to continue a nursing career she had temporarily put aside when we got married. I thought of the gifts my wife Marvel had brought to Mizpah High School, teaching business and music classes, acting as school nurse and the accompanist for the student choirs. Was there someone out there who could fill all of those very important shoes?

My children were approaching college age, yet they certainly did not want to leave Micronesia, They loved it there and had become well acclimated. The island young folk were all very warm and friendly and it was exciting for my children to learn and become a part of the island culture of the young Micronesians.

I felt relieved when word came from the Mission Board that they had located a couple to take our place. The board urged us to take our

Mizpah students

well-deserved year of furlough, which was the customary way of reviving long-term missionaries. That year could be used in service, traveling around the country promoting the work of the mission, but could also be used for advanced studies.

Our decision was made and we packed our bags, leaving all of our furniture behind for our replacement family who would simply move into our apartment. The piano was the hardest to part with as it had come with us all the way from Vermont.

Saying goodbye to loved ones is never a happy time. I can still recall the sight of Marm and Dad trying to hold back their tears while waving good-bye to me as I headed off to war. I didn't say it, but at the time I was quite certain I would not be coming back.

This time I had to say goodbye to my Micronesian friends. I was headed home to Maine again, but I had mixed feelings. Yes, I was very happy to be able to see Marm and Dad again. I loved my work in Micronesia. We had been a family, a happy family, and a loving family. I truly believe we taught our students more than mere educational skills. My teachers and supporting staff, all who came to me with no former experience, carried out their tasks with joy and plentiful skills. We brought them a new way of living, one that would extend out to their people in the new world that was to be theirs. I had come to love my students. I had chosen them. They had been ideal students, and I felt privileged to have taught them.

The school year had come to a close. We had to make a hurried departure to attend Paula's graduation in Hawaii. Our students were making ready to leave for their island homes. Some of my staff were preparing for summer vacations, while others had completed their terms and would soon be leaving for good too. There was no time for a big farewell party. We loaded up a group of departing staff and students into our small bus and headed to the airport. After the flurry of excitement and goodbyes we boarded the plane.

From the windows of the plane we took one last look at our little island home. I thought of how it all began, touring the island with Tuck Wah Lee in those first days of our island life. We had been so amazed by all we saw. I felt so overwhelmed by all the work I knew was set before me. It seemed like a daunting task to start a school called Mizpah. Yet, we had done it. We had created a bright beacon of hope for the people of Micronesia. We had built, not just a school and the buildings that go with it, but we had also helped the young people to become their own beacons of hope for others.

For us, it had been an adventure none of us would ever forget. The connections we made at Mizpah, and the different world we had been a part of for the last five years, these lasting influences we carried with us across the Pacific to Maine. It was an experience that continued to shape us for years to come.

Many Christians have looked to the biblical story of Mizpah and seen it as a parting blessing, known as the Mizpah Benediction, and associate it with a safe return. I didn't know if I would ever return to Truk or Micronesia. I didn't know what would become of the school we worked so hard to build, or how the lives of the students would play out in the future. Would they become the leaders of Micronesia? Would they finally take charge of their own destiny and shake off the hold of the superpowers? I felt confident that they would.

As the tiny dots of the Truk islands faded from my view through the plane window I sent my Mizpah blessing down to those I had connected with over those five years, "May God bless you and keep you."

The very long journey home to Maine from Micronesia was quite tiring, but as we descended the plane Portland, Maine never looked so good. There were Dad and Marm with tears in their eyes and big smiles on their faces, three of my sisters, my two brothers, numerous nieces and nephews, and several family friends. It was a welcoming I had never expected. I knew then that I never wanted to leave Maine again.

Micronesia Comes to Maine

My boyhood experiences in the Maine woods taught me that all trails lead somewhere. They may come to an end, but at least you are in a different place than where you started. After five years of following the missionary trail I found myself once again trying to determine which way to go next.

My personal desire had always been to live in a rural setting with plenty of elbowroom, where I could grow my own food, cut my own firewood, and live to enjoy all of the things I so enjoyed in my boyhood. Dreams do come true sometimes. I can still hear the real estate agent telling me all the reasons why I probably would not want to purchase a particular home in Norway, Maine. It was an abandoned 40-acre farm in very bad condition, with a fallen barn, and fields full of brush and weeds. There was no indoor plumbing, electricity or heating system in the 1887 home. However, I knew I could put my carpentry skills to work again and renovate the buildings. It was the prospect of 40 acres of woods and fields that deeply appealed to my imagination. The asking price was ridiculously low; only $20,000. Then she mentioned the owner wanted to get rid of it and would probably take a lower price. I thought the property should be worth more, but I made what I thought was an absurd offer of just $13,000.

Haying at Fitikoko Farm, Paul in truck, Susan and Alan pitching bales

SOLD! I "bought the farm." We moved in the middle of the summer, which gave me plenty of time to winterize the house and look for employment at nearby schools.

Not long after buying the house I ventured across the mountain pass to the small town of Buckfield. I came upon the modest building of Buckfield High School. I was about to enter the building when a gentleman came out of the main door. I asked him if the principal might be inside. "No," he told me, "but I'm the superintendent." After a short conversation with the superintendent I was immediately hired as the mathematics and science teacher of Buckfield High School.

While I waited for the school year to begin I continued working as a traveling agent helping to drum up support for the mission programs. I was giving weekly presentations to churches about missionary work and the story of Mizpah. With each talk my love for my students stayed very much alive. Fresh memories of them were still deep in my heart, and I wished I could still do something for them.

I think I saw a blinking star right over the farm one night. I know it really didn't happen, but a message hit my brain. I could bring some of the students to Maine to live with us for a few years. I could help them finish high school right here in Norway and then see them on to higher education.

I gave the idea a lot of deep thinking and praying and discussion with my family. The idea seemed to have two sides. There certainly would be plenty of positives. They could experience a whole *new* world, and seek higher education in the States. The other side of this idea was that they would be away from their island home for a long time, something many Micronesians with ambitions had to do. The hope was that they would return to their islands and become leaders for their people.

My family was highly in favor of the idea and we quickly decided that we could take care of at least three of the students from Mizpah. Our own children would be finishing their high school years right alongside the island youths, and they already knew each other, which would make us one big happy family.

I quickly sent off a letter to the staff at Mizpah asking them to recommend three freshman-level youths. The faculty arranged for the entire freshman student class to write an essay on why they would love to take on such a venture. The search came to a swift result and I soon was planning for the transportation of a girl named Markari and her brother, Jack, and one other boy by the name of Ritis. The faculty provided airfare for the students from their own personal funds and made certain they would have all the proper clothing for our sterner climate. Since none of the three had ever traveled by air, and would have to make three or four flight changes before landing, the faculty provided a chaperone to see the youths all the way to Maine. I was overjoyed when we met them at the Portland Airport and brought them to Norway, Maine.

The next four years of my life were once again some of the busiest times but also some of the happiest times of my life. The young lady, named Markari Jack, was a very sweet girl, bubbling with life, very intelligent and eager to learn anything that came her way. Her brother Jack Jack had been chosen to come with her because the family wanted her to have protection. Jack was also a very sharp-minded young boy, somewhat quieter than Markari, who enjoyed all kinds of physical

Dinner at Fitikoko Farm with (left to right) a school friend, Jack Jack, Paul, Paul's father Henry Marshall, Paula, and Susan

activity. Our third youth, Ritis Heldart, was very eager to learn every-thing about his new life and was always asking questions about everything around him.

When our Micronesian youths settled in they gave the farm a fitting new name: *Fitikoko*, which in Trukese means: "Everything normal, all fouled up." It certainly fit our years there on the farm, as we had so many interesting things going on all of the time.

All three of them enjoyed being a part of the family and helping with every phase of living. The boys were excited about the farm, land, and the woods. They were eager to learn about cutting and preparing firewood, starting a vegetable garden, and helping me renovate the old farm build-ings. With the boys' help and eagerness we actually built a new barn.

During their first year I had the good fortune to purchase four riding horses. The horses had seen better years but they still had enough life to give us all the pleasures of saddling them up and riding all over our 40 acres. I think learning to ride horseback was one of the most enjoyable activities the boys had. Both of them took it upon themselves to learn to ride saddle-less, bareback.

My three new teenagers joined in well at the high school and soon were singing in the school choir and taking part in many other activities. They easily made friends with the local students, and the teachers reported to me very often how much they enjoyed having the Micronesian kids in their classes.

Ritis and Jack helping to build a new barn at Fitikoko

Soon my eager island folk learned the joys of Maine winters. At first they were worried about how they would keep warm when the temperatures went low. It did not take them long to figure out that you have to dress for the cold in Maine. You can't just dash outdoors with little coverings as they did back in their warm homeland. They often helped me shovel snow. They especially enjoyed the wood stoves we used to heat the house. In our second year, they helped me construct a huge stone fireplace, which became a favorite spot to spend the evening doing homework.

After school the three of them could hardly wait to get on their sleds and free ride down our long steep hill. They learned to ski, and soon after that to snowshoe. To top it all off, I purchased two old-time sleighs and neighborhood children as well as adults, who heard about our *Fitikoko Farm*, came up our hillside to enjoy our winter playground.

The next three years found us involved in graduations, and then the exodus. They all began to leave home as they chose their paths to further education. Markari entered a nurses training course. Her brother Jack chose a criminal justice training course, and Ritis won a full scholarship to a college in Nebraska. My own children were moving on as well. My daughter Paula completed her nurses training and moved some distance from home. Susan attended a college in Maine, while my son Alan, the youngest, joined the United States Navy and was often very far from home.

The two boys, Ritis and Jack, returned to their island homes and both became leaders in their new country, the Federated States of Micronesia. Jack was chosen as the first head of the Criminal Justice branch, and Ritis was recently elected governor of what we used to call Truk, now the newly-formed state of Chuuk.

With the help of the Internet I have traced down the names of many of my Mizpah students and am not surprised to learn that many of them are serving in major leadership positions (for the full list see the appendix). Reviewing this list I cannot help but feel that the goal I set, "to prepare Christian leaders for their new world," had been accomplished.

Then something unexpected happened. My son, Alan, and Markari developed a caring relationship with one another, which blossomed after they left home. They informed me they were in love and wanted to get married. I could think of nothing that would please me more, as I loved both of them very much, and a marriage between them, so I thought, would keep them both very close to me. Sadly, that did not happen quite that way. Alan's term in the Navy took him far way into the Pacific and I saw very little of them for the next several years.

The result of their marriage provided me with four wonderful American-Micronesian grandchildren, which later provided me with six great-grandchildren, as of last count. Through them, our connection to Micronesia continues even to this day.

The Last Class of Mizpah High

In 1972 the Mission Board decided to close Mizpah High School. It was the end of an era. Even though the school did not last as long as we had hoped, the impact we had made on the lives of the people and students of Micronesia would continue to ripple into the future. That May, Marvel and I returned to Truk for the final graduation. The following is my speech to the graduating class:

Address to the graduates of the class of 1972, Mizpah High School of Micronesia, May 25, 1972:

I want to convey to you the intense feeling of appreciation for the great honor of being a part of this memorable occasion. My wife and I have traveled over 8,500 miles back into a dream that began for me in April 1963. This is an opportunity that seldom comes to anyone, to be able to reenter a beautiful dream and bring it to a happy ending.

I can remember when this very ground on which we are now seated was just a jungle; a small stream running out of a spring just above us, where each day the women of the village came to do their washing. The ground where the girl's dormitory is now standing was a cemetery. The baseball field and the tennis court was a swamp, which we filled in to create a playground area. I can remember the first men who came to begin the construction of the buildings, volunteers from the islands of Namoneus and Faichuk. I can recall the morning when the cargo ship Serina docked at Baker Dock, and for three days and nights we unloaded cargo, the boards, and the cement, and the doors and windows, the nails and the bolts, that finally became the beautiful place where we now are gathered.

But I am not here tonight to eulogize a building or a tennis court, or a baseball field, or dormitories or classrooms. Those are all things of passing value, sparkling for a while and then losing their shine and glitter. Their true value is derived only from the spirit that has been generated here; a spirit that grows stronger and spreads itself throughout the universe.

Tonight, I would like to create for you an analogy, likening the dream of Mizpah to the conquest of space. Centuries ago a man by the name of Leonardo Da Vinci designed the first airplane on paper. It was never built, because it was just a dream that men thought was impossible, but the seed was planted and would eventually lift man off the surface of the earth. Later on, air balloons actually did lift man from the ground. Then the Wright brothers built an airplane with an engine that could take men wherever they wanted to go. The rocket engine was finally invented, with sufficient power to boost men out of the gravitational pull of the earth, giving them the freedom of the heavens. He was finally free, free to explore, free to venture forth into unknown moons and planets, to probe into the very depths of God's universe. The mysteries of eternity began to be revealed to him. There was no end to his vision.

But when astronauts who took part in the Apollo missions were asked what were their most profound impressions during their trip into space, it turned out that their deepest emotions had been to see the earth from outer space. The astronauts were over-whelmed by the beauty of the earth as compared with the bleakness of space and the grayness of the moon.

The incredible beauty of the earth as seen from space results largely from the fact that our planet is covered with living things. What gives vibrant colors and exciting variety to the surface of the earth is the fact that it is literally a living organism.

The idea that this earth upon which we live is unique and different from any other place we will be able to discover, is not a scientific fact as yet, but it is a fact that the great master of the entire cosmos saw fit to create a small portion of his infinite heavens something different than that which he placed anywhere else, something that was so unique, so precious, so immensely wonderful – life! No matter how far we travel, no matter how many planets we explore, the earth, the source of our life, our home, will always look the best to us. The sad part of it is that we will have to view it from a different perspective before we come to the realization of its beauty.

Not too long ago, as time and space are concerned, you took your first steps into space. You heard and dreamed of a world outside of your homeland. All you needed was a way to get there. A way was provided for you. The great rocket ship called Mizpah High School was constructed, and you came on board, becoming astronauts. You have gone through your training period, as all space travelers must do, and now you are listening to the countdown. Tomorrow you will blast off, heading at vast speeds to new worlds, exploring, wondering, fearing, to experience thrilling and exciting new lives. In just a short while you will be leaving behind you the initial rocket engine, which has furnished you with the power to break the forces of gravity that have held you here. The great rocket engine, Mizpah High School, is no longer needed. She has done her job for you. You are now free to wander in space, to go wherever your mind and your ambitions will take you. Nothing can stop you, except your own foolishness, your own lack of sense of duty, your own lack of ambition, or perhaps your own selfish desire to go where you are going alone. For no man will be able to travel through this world or the world of space alone. For one thing, he would not be able to withstand the loneliness that he would have to suffer. You may think that now you have the knowledge necessary you can go on to new worlds alone, but in so thinking you forget from whence comes your sense of power.

A rocket ship cannot travel through space without a vast number of people back on the earth, assisting them with their controls, providing them with data and information necessary for them to do their exploring. There must be behind them many people. Were it not for those people your travel would be an impossible thing. The same is true for you. When you leave here you must remember that the source of your power is not where you are going, but where you came from. The source of your life is not out there, but right here, because the real source is not money, ships, land, or clothes, but the love of the people who have sacrificed so much that you might be able to venture forth, that you might have clothes to wear, that you might have a chance to learn. Your source of power, your great rocket engine, Mizpah High School, derived its power from the love, which hundreds and thousands of people gave, that you might be among the first to explore new worlds. Your source of power has been your teachers, your parents, and the men who worked so hard to give you your school, your churches, and people from far off countries who believed in you.

Let us not forget also that your source of power began many years ago.

Right here on this very spot, just 200 feet from where you now sit, lies the foundation of the temporary home of the Rev. Robert Logan, the first missionary, whose dream was to set you free to explore. Just across the lagoon on the island of Dublon lies Rev. Logan's remains and a monument stands in memory of his gift to you and your people.

Up on the hill behind us lies the foundation of the first girls school in Truk, where your mother's mothers studied that you also might learn, that your lives would be enriched with love for one another. There are examples all over your islands of the work and the dreams of hundreds of your own people, their hopes and their prayers, their sweat and their muscles, that you and future generations of your children might come to know a Spirit that would give you the power to overcome this earth and all of its evils.

The dream of Mizpah was not a singular purpose; it was not merely to give you a high school education. The closing of Mizpah is just another chapter, another scene played out in the dream designed to help people create a better world.

There will be a great deal of sadness in your hearts as you leave this beautiful place that has been your home for these past years, but there will also be a great deal of happiness in recalling the thousands of wonderful times you have had here. You will look back, year after year, and still see the faces of your teachers who gave you their knowledge and shared their hopes and dreams as they prepared you for the world that you are now entering as you leave here.

You have begun to take part in a new discovery, a discovery of your selves, who you are, where you belong, where you are going.

Let's take a moment to consider the first of those discoveries, Who Are You? Now don't make the mistake that you are *just you*. Don't be so foolish to take all of the credit for what you have become, because, if you had to depend entirely on yourself you would really be nothing. You are, first of all, what God made you to be. That you have to accept and make the best of every attribute that God gave you. You are, secondly, every thing your parents succeeded in making you to be. You are the result of their love, their worries, and their care of you when you were sick. You are a result of the long hours and the hard work of the men who built Mizpah High School. You are the dream of Rev. Robert Logan, and every missionary who lived and died that you might be free to live and to love. You are the result of your teachers, those who led you before you came to Mizpah High School, and recently those missionary teachers and the Peace Corps young men and women, whose desire it was to leave their homes and bring to you their love to help you to find a better life in a changing world.

You are a new spirit of Micronesia, molded and created by every person who ever had a vision for your people.

You are the astronauts who will make new discoveries, explore new heavens, seeking out ways and worlds. But you will be making a big mistake if you think that it is all for yourselves. For "no man is an island unto himself." That is a phrase from a poem by the great English poet John Dunne in which he wrote: "no man is an island of itself. Every man is part of the continent, part of the main." You are a part and portion of all from whence you have sprung. You will be a part of all of the new worlds to which you are going.

This brings me to the second question: Where are you going? This I cannot tell you in detail, for I am not a fortune teller or a soothsayer, but this I know, you are going out into a world that is the most beautiful, the most wonderful, and the most exciting place you could ever imagine. You are also going into a world that is the saddest, most evil, and the sickest of places that even your dreams could not create. God created the world the first way. Man has made it the second way, and it is all yours to do whatever you will with it. You can work to restore it, to rebuild it, to regenerate the beauty. You can turn it into a heaven or you can turn it into the dirtiest, rottenest, sickest, most filthy and vile place. You can turn it into a Hell.

Just remember this. The place where you are going will be whatever you make it, nothing more, nothing less. The choice is yours. The challenge is yours!

Yes, you are the explorers. Your rocket ship may carry you out to far distant places, cities and countries that until now you have only read of, or it may carry you only to some faraway island. You may see spectacular sights, even presidents and kings. You may be thrilled and dazzled by the sights and the lights, by the promise of wealth, by the possibilities of self-glory. But I am more inclined to believe that you will be more like those in the poem written by another poet, T. S. Eliot in his poem, "The Four Quartets."

We shall not cease from exploration
And the end of all our exploring
Will be to arrive where we started
And know the place for the first time.

Your search will be for happiness, but you will learn that happiness cannot be found somewhere else, but right where you are, at any given time. Beauty is not out there; it is right here in your own heart. Life is not out there; it is right within you, wherever you are.

The third discovery that you will make is: Where do you belong? Now some of you might want to take the proud, self-praising way and say that you belong to no place, that you belong to no one, that you have gotten where you are by your own efforts, or that you belong to Micronesia or Truk or Ponepei. But you are wrong. First of all you belong to the earth. Perhaps your roots are in Micronesia, but your branches gained their nourishment from the entire earth. You belong to the land, you belong to the sea, and you belong to all of the people on the earth for they are your brothers and sisters. You are all a part of the same family. You do not belong to yourselves, but to the world. Therefore every motive you have should be to use every talent, all of your energies, for the benefit of those people and places to whom you belong.

You may accumulate great knowledge, but it is not yours for the keeping. You may gather great wealth, but it not yours to use selfishly. You have a great responsibility to life itself, to restore it wherever it is being destroyed, to revive it, to generate it. You must not desecrate or destroy life in any form, without replacing it. If you use the land you must replenish it. If you are a part of the millions who pollute the waters and the air, then you must be willing to pay the price of restoring its purity. If you derive your livelihood from society, then you must do all in your power to improve and constantly rebuild it to the ideal state. You must supply it with new ideas, new contributions, and new discoveries. Your task in life is not to see how high up the ladder you can climb; it is to help all you can along the way.

The end of your journey will eventually bring you back home, wherever that may be, and for the first time you will see that everything you always wanted was right there all the time. You will see that there is just as much beauty wherever you are as you wish to see. You will see that there is just as much work to do for others as you wish to do. You will see that there is just as much pain and suffering, dying and living everywhere, just as much trouble, and just as much happiness. You will find God just as certainly there along the shore as you will find Him in any great cathedral in Europe or anywhere else. At the end of it all you will find the world and all that is there within, is just whatever you make it.

We are facing another moment of eternity tonight. We are closing the covers of another great book, one of only a few short, but memorable, chapters. It is up to you whether or not this book becomes a great classic that remains alive and constantly grows better as it grows older. That spirit has already taken new roots in places like Silliman University in the Philippines, in the University of Guam, of Hawaii, the University of Oregon, California, Mansfield College, Seminaries, junior colleges, agricultural schools, technical schools, businesses here in Micronesia, and classrooms where some of our graduates are already teaching others.

To some people there is sadness because they think we have come to the end of a beautiful dream, one that was cut short because we awoke too soon, but to me Mizpah High School was bigger than all of that. There was a spirit of Mizpah that was created on the day that we first broke ground here. It was carried on when the men of Micronesia built this school. It grew stronger when our first class graduated and went off into the world, and it is still spreading wherever you, I, and all of those who gave a part of their lives to Mizpah, live up to the standards that we found here. To me, the closing of Mizpah is not the end of a dream, but the beginning of a greater one, and you are a part of it.

My advice to you is to live and love every minute of your lives. Love everyone that you come in contact with. Be not suspicious of anyone but give your love to that person first, that he or she might feel that love and be able to return that love to you. You are a very important part of God's great and eternal kingdom. You belong to God and his earth and to all of the people on earth. You are going into the world to discover its beauty, its sadness, and to restore the beauty of life wherever you may go.

As we part, I can think of no better blessing than that found in the Bible known as the Mizpah Blessing: "May the Lord watch between me and thee while we are absent one from another." Amen

Epilogue

As a young boy, when we lived on the Cunningham farm in Patten, every Sunday we walked four miles into town for Sunday school, even during winter. Marm led the way, followed by us kids in order of our age. One of the neighbor farmwomen said my mother looked like an old mother hen, leading us to God, with her chickens following her. I was the last one in line, and my legs were also the shortest. In the wintertime I could be hauled on a sled, which of course I truly loved. Sometimes I would even fall asleep on that sled. My mother taught Sunday school. My father never went to church because he was always working, but we always went. It was joy. We all just loved to go. It was a Methodist church. We learned a lot about the Bible. There was no pressure, no talk about sin. It was a wonderful place to sing together and have games.

The only pastors I ever knew were student ministers from Bangor Theological Seminary. They would come on Friday nights and stay through Sunday. My mother often took them in during their visits to our town and provided room and board. We had one student minister, Travers Smith, who stayed with us on weekends for two years. He was like a brother to me and I wanted to help him and the other ministers. Travers served another church 15 miles away and I would go with him in his car to be his right-hand man.

Much later in my life, after my Micronesian missionary adventure, Travers advised me on my final occupational journey, of which I have not gone into detail here in this book, the path of a Christian Minister. For the last 40 years I served many churches in my home state of Maine.

Throughout my life I have taken the road less traveled, and that has made all the difference.

Paul E. Marshall, a Maine Boy

Appendix

Even though Mizpah High School is no longer operating, its legacy remains. Here a few examples of how some of the students, from the classes of 1969 and 1970, have had an impact on the Federated States of Micronesia (FSM). This is not an exhaustive list and was taken from information available on the internet. Omissions and errors are regretted.

Ishmael Dobich – Public Affairs Officer of the State of Chuuk; National Election Commission-Chuuk; National Election Consultant-Chuuk; Deputy Secretary of the Department of Foreign Affairs-FSM; Consul General to Hawaii-FSM

Akissy Edward – Quarantine Officer-Chuuk

Rev. Russell Edwards – Associate Member-Pacific Islands Health Officers Association (PIHOA); Acting Assistant Secretary-PIHOA; Ministry of Health Republic of the Marshall Islands (RMI); Assistant Secretary of Primary Health Care; Hospital Administrator

Rev. Bender Enicar – Pastor; President of United Church of Christ-Pohnpei; Member of Pohnpei Legislature; Administrator of Youth and Social Affairs-Pohnpei State

Edigar Isaac – Task Force on the special referendum for proposed amendment submitted by the Third Constitutional Convention-FSM, Vice Chair-Pohnpei; Assistant Secretary-Department of Finance and Administration for the establishment of FSM's Embassy in Beijing, Office of Personnel-FSM; National Biodiversity Strategy and Action Plan Steering Committee-FSM; Public Awareness and Engagement Committee-Pohnpei Strategic Development Plan

Rev. Palukne Johnny – Pastor, Southern Association of the Southern California/Nevada Conference of the UCC; Pastor, San Diego Marshallese Church; Pastor, Southwest Conference UCC

Banuel Sailas – Health Statistician-Chuuk; Chief of Medical Records and Statistics, Department of Health Services-Weno, Chuuk

Youser Anson – Historic Preservation Officer-Pohnpei, Department of Land and Natural Resources

Honorable Henry Asugar – Journalist; Editor; Interpreter; Administrative Assistant-Chuuk State Congregational Delegation; Longest serving Chief Clerk of the FSM Congress; Floor Leader of 13th Congress

Karson Enlet – Special Assistant of Legislative Affairs-FSM; A leader in the movement for separation of Faichuk from the State of Chuuk and its establishment as a separate republic-In the 1980's Faichuk voted for commonwealth status.; Executive Director at Chuuk State Healthcare Plan

Alvin Jacklick – Minister of Internal Affairs; Health and Environment-Nauru; Senator-FSM; Member Joint RMI/FSM Congressional Staff

Carl Jeadrik – Administrator, Ministry of Education-FSM

Johnny Killion – Micronesian Maritime Authority; Board of Directors; Owner of a Print Shop

Redley Killion – State Resources and Development Director; Board of Directors of the FSM Petroleum Corporation; Vice President, two terms, FSM

Ritas Heldart – Governor, State of Chuuk

Dr. Winston Likiaksa – Kusrae Hospital-Otolaryngology; National Scholarship Board for FSM; Pohnpei State Department of Health Services

Also associated with the school were:

Jack J. Jack – Chief of the Division of Security and Investigation-FSM; Assistant Postmaster-Pohnpei

Danny Leopold – Coordinator of Post-Secondary Education-FSM

Marstella Jack – First Attorney General-FSM; Micronesian Conservation Trust; Pohnpei Women's Advisory Council-FSM; Pacific Concerns Resources Center, Board of Directors; Principal Legal Advisor-Pohnpei E.P.A.; Civil Society Advisory Group; FSM Cabinet Member; Delegate United Nations 23rd Special Session on Women

Magdalina Walter – First woman Senator-Pohnpei State Congress; First woman Chairperson 8th Pohnpei Legislature

ACKNOWLEDGMENTS

I would like to thank my wife, Linda Campbell-Marshall, and my friend, Jennifer Curran, for the love, help, and support they gave me during the process of putting this book together. I would especially like to thank Meghan Vigeant, my "personal historian," for her guidance and encouragement.